MOUNTAINEER
MARRIAGE

A Proven Guide to Developing A
Strong And Healthy Marriage

D. Deshazer

First Printing: 2020

ISBN: 9798666138632

Copy Editor:
Melinda Hicks

Cover design by: Fabrice Villard

ACKNOWLEDGMENT

I would like to acknowledge my parents, Archie and Tonya Hensley for the love and support during the time of completing Mountaineer Marriage. As some may know, it is not easy to maintain consistency in completing any form of a manuscript. But through their encouragement and motivation, I was able to create something that I know will change lives and heal marriages!

It's hard to imagine how the outcome of my marriage would have been, had it not been for my friend and mentor, Marvin Jinx, coming to our rescue. Tia and I prayed for some sort of help with reconciling our marriage. Sure enough, and out of know where, Marvin contacted me on LinkedIn to see how I was doing. Had he not intervened, I'm not sure Tia and I would be together now. I am truly grateful for the time he spent, by helping us fight for healing. Prayer answered!

I can honestly say it's challenging to find supportive people now and days outside of family. When I went to facebook to find an experienced Ice climber, a few people said they would help, but it was Charly Oliver, an experienced rock climber that took the initiative and reached out to me via Facebook messenger. Because of him, I was able to gain a decent amount of mountaineering knowledge to create a comparison between marriage and mountaineering.

PREFACE

By reading this book, you will learn how to equip your marriage with the proper principles for maintaining healthy relationships by having a mountaineering mindset. You will also learn to take life's most serious choices, more seriously. This is how you can become Mountaineers, as it were, on an expedition for a much stronger union.

MARRIAGE RESOURCES

Congratulations on your decision to embark on a new journey within your marriage. This book is designed to be used as a tool to enhance, enrich and restore the foundation of your marriage. The program was developed with the intention of using a personal story and analogy to inspire and change the scope of marriages around the world.

Remember as you go through this book that there is a workbook available to assist in the process, with each module being based on the contents of this book. We are with you every step of the way and hope you find comfort and enjoyment as you work through the modules and chapters.

We understand that some marriages need 1-on-1 assistance to work through the modules and we provide professional marriage coaching for those who are in need. You can schedule a free consultation at (www.mountaineermarriage.com) by clicking the Link "Coaching".

"Wishing you a life-changing climb up the Mountaineer Marriage!"

CONTENTS

1. THE EXPEDITION

I t takes an extraordinary level of bravery to climb a mountain. You have to be physically as well as mentally tough. This is no easy stroll! But those who make the choice to embark on an expedition up a 29,000 ft mountain are committed and passionate. Their reasons are myriad; for some, it's the adrenaline rush, for others, it's about conquering fear. The common thread that stretches between mountain climbers is that they understand the risks involved but take every precaution to thrive and survive on this life-affirming trip.

Sunrise Mountain stands high on the east side of Las Vegas with an elevation of 3,363ft. It's one of the most recognizable landmarks seen from the valley of the city. When I lived with my aunt and uncle for a short period of time in order to attend a performing arts high school, I would gaze upon the glory of Sunrise Mountain on my walk home from school every day. The mountain loomed like a jagged goliath in the distance, growing ever taller and more imposing the closer I got.

One day, my friend and I decided we should take a journey up the mountain. Sunrise Mountain was a popular hiking destination but we really didn't know much about it. How hard could it be? Impulsively, we each grabbed a light bag, some water and a snack, and set off on our quest. We didn't make a plan; we didn't do any research. We didn't even ask my aunt and uncle where we should start or physically map out a path. We simply took off with the mountain in our sights.

At first, climbing the mountain was exhilarating and fun. At several points along the way, we found ourselves jumping from one rock to another like a scene from a movie. We figured that by doing our ascent that way, it would be quicker and more exciting. But soon, we looked up to see that we still had a very long way to go. To make matters worse, the incline was clearly becoming steeper.

My friend and I walked for what seemed like hours on end, and eventually we were pretty much free-climbing the mountain with no training and more worryingly, no gear. We decided to try to switch routes, making a course change in the opposite direction. But the path we chose stopped suddenly. I looked over the ledge and saw that the drop was horrifying. We realized with our hearts in our throats that we had ventured into a dangerous area where we weren't supposed to climb. Many people had successfully hiked this mountain and had made it all the way to the top. Why was it so hard for us?

Being stubborn and perhaps a little naive, we continued to climb further. The path became more precipitous; at one point, we were leaping over huge gaps in an attempt to climb the mountain. When it finally dawned on me that I was staring death in the face, I told my friend it wasn't safe for us to continue. He concurred, and I think he was relieved I had spoken up. You know it had to be rough if two teenage boys agreed something was dangerous!

We had looked forward to the view of the valley and the powerful feeling of accomplishment from the climb. Now we would feel lucky to make it down the mountain in one piece. Our current location made one thing clear: heading back down that steep section of the mountain was not an option. We had been jumping from rock to rock on our way up, but doing that in reverse was too dangerous. The ground beneath us wasn't all that stable, forcing us to slow down so we didn't slip or outright fall. As we descended at one point, I came across an incredibly steep drop. A wiser man would have found a safer way down. Of course, this was not one of my best decision-making days and after all, teenage boys are invincible. I decided to go for it; I took aim and lept off. Unfortunately, I hit the ground hard, landed at a bad angle, and sprained my ankle. I limped the rest of the way down the mountain and all the way home.

What does mountain climbing have to do with marriage? Well, I had the summit of Sunrise Mountain in my sights, had heard the success stories, saw the joy on the faces of those who reveled in their own treks, and I wanted more than anything to stand atop that mountain. However, I failed to learn anything about it. I didn't bother to research the proper and safest routes, didn't even ask my aunt which path to take. I bit off far more than I could chew because my desire to get to the summit was greater than my willingness to learn how to safely make the journey. Ultimately, I took on a difficult challenge in total ignorance.

Most of us marvel at the idea of marriage. We desire to commit our life to someone, forge a robust, lifelong bond with a partner. This is the summit in our sights. Yet, we most often lack any sort of real understanding or knowledge of what it takes to make a marriage work. We start out strong but stop educating ourselves along the journey, causing us to stumble as the pathways change.

From the comfort of my aunt and uncle's home, it seemed very possible - perhaps, almost easy - to make it up Sunrise Mountain. But in the midst of the dangerous terrain, our lack of training, preparation and knowledge caused us to fail miserably. We had to come back down far earlier than we expected, without ever experiencing all the joy of being on the top of the mountain. In marriage, many of us come so close to victory but fall short because we don't have the right tools for the journey. Led by fear, we forget that preparation and faith supersede doubt.

Although I only suffered a sprained ankle, I endured significant pain from my mistake. With marriage, unplanned injuries can result in divorce – and considerable pain.. When we call it quits and end a marriage, it causes hurt for both spouses; it also affects everyone around us, whether we know it or not.

I could offer you some well-researched statistics on the divorce rate in the United States, but that is not my area of expertise. Generally speaking, it is said that roughly half of all marriages end in divorce. Those are frightening odds. However, I'd rather spend my time and energy on figuring out solutions to prevent such negative results. Although I realize that some marriage statistics are essential in terms of understanding society's position and outlook on marriage, we need to shift our focus toward our goals as opposed to how likely we will fail to achieve them.

Tony Hawk, arguably one of the greatest skateboarders of all time, once said that when he leans into a halfpipe; he puts all his force forward, toward the slope. Tony said that if he resists even just a little, by stepping back in the opposite direction that he is going, he's in danger of falling completely off the board. Likewise, a rock climber focuses more on the summit and their ascent than they do on staring down at the bottom of the mountain, risking fear and negative thoughts.

I set out with a simple objective for this book: to teach people how to refocus their minds when it comes to having a strong and healthy marriage. I want to help my readers lean forward onto that halfpipe and only look upward. I genuinely believe that the more you focus on something, the more you will be drawn to it. So, if we can all begin treating our marriages like climbing a mountain, we will better equip ourselves mentally and even spiritually.

Like you, my wife and I often see our married friends on social media, sharing happy images, which can look quite glamorous and realistic. However, we all know that there are genuine struggles behind those beautiful scenes. And they, and perhaps even you, have forgotten or never even knew what it takes to make a marriage work, or how to fight to save one. When you follow what we have laid out in this book, you will find yourself fully equipped to tackle and climb over any issues that threaten your marriage. With these tools, I sincerely hope you will realize that saving your marriage is a battle of spiritual warfare. You can own your marriage, and together we change the statistics of divorce, one marriage at a time.

2. LEARN THE MOUNTAIN

The traverse of Gasherbrum I

Gasherbrum I, also known as Hidden Peak, is one of the world's highest mountains, at 8080 meters (26,510 ft.) above sea level, putting it at the 11th tallest on record. The Traverse Of Hidden Peak has been done just once, in 1975, by Reinhold Messner and Peter Habeler. Only really experienced mountaineers try a peak as difficult as Gasherbrum, which is why this mountain has fewer deaths than the more infamous Mount Everest. This particular mountain is unique, thanks to its remote location in the highest peaks of the Karakoram.

We've all heard stories comparing marriage to going to war, roller coasters, and even a deck of cards. No one, to my knowledge, has ever compared it to climbing an ice mountain. Once this thought occurred to me, I couldn't stop thinking that it's a perfect comparison. With one caveat: this is no ordinary mountain, it's more like an ice mountain. Slippery, treacherous, a trek that needs the utmost concentration, preparation and precaution. Think of it in those terms and we'll be far more careful with our spouse in every area of our relationship.

Full disclosure, I'm on my second and lifelong marriage. So, I know firsthand what it is like to fail at marriage, and all of the heartache and self-punishing one endures because of it. Ironically, prior to my first marriage, I spent a lot of time educating myself about marriage. I knew that one day, I wanted to find a lifelong partner, and I needed to make sure I knew what was expected of me in the marriage. I learned about the art of conflict resolution, the various types of intimacy, and the particular way the brain functions in marriage versus singleness. What I failed to realize is that this should have been a continuing education after I said "I do." I thought that the knowledge with which I entered into my marriage would carry me through a lifelong commitment, and to my surprise, I was very wrong.

No matter how long we've known our partner, nor how many hours of research we've completed, marriage is a journey that requires constant education. As time passes, we will all deal with different problems, new seasons, and challenging scenarios in life. Therefore, it's crucial that we have more modern tools and multiple approaches in which we can handle various issues. Relationships in which partners stop learning often turn stagnant, and that staleness can lead to the marriage becoming dull and lifeless, potentially inviting a lot of other unwanted issues.

By the time my friend and I realized that we traveled up Sunrise Mountain the wrong way, on that path to nowhere, we were too tired to go all the way back down and start back up in the right direction. The hike had exhausted us and left us feeling defeated. Sadly, we never tried to hike Sunrise Mountain again.

My fear for many first-time marriages is that the husband and wife will dive into it, not fully understanding what it takes to build a strong, unbreakable bond. Then, after the inevitable arguments, one of you has said the word 'divorce', or suggested that you separate, and both partners have become mentally and physically exhausted. It will take more strength and effort to fix what has been broken than to provide maintenance during a time of peace.

Another way to understand the importance of marital education is to know how it is viewed in today's marriage-illiterate society. The lack of proper and consistent marriage education has separated us from knowing the true purpose behind the Godly creation of marriage. We can simply categorize this misunderstanding by breaking marriages into two forms: contract vs. covenant. This is a vital part of understanding the desires, goals, and aspirations that you set for you and your partner. Whether you are planning to be married or well into your marriage journey, this is critical information. The foundation that your marriage rests upon should be well established so that you can build upon it over a lifetime.

Contract Marriage

In today's age, when it comes to marriage, most people have a contract perspective. It's a purely transactional approach, and that transactional approach signifies only a subtle shift in our perspective. When any contract is created, the parties promise to abide by a written legal agreement, enforceable by law. When a contract is breached, the loyal party can take legal action against the party to whom it breached. This is the action in which a spouse can declare grounds for divorce. Marriage as a contract becomes a carefully constructed agreement between husband and wife.

Contracts are formed to be wholly technical and straight by the books. When we walk into a marital commitment with this mindset, we subconsciously condition our minds to focus on the technical aspects of a marriage instead of its spiritual purpose. We set unreasonable standards, intentionally or not, and expect them all to be met. But when our standards are not kept, we find legal reasons to justify an escape from our obligations or commitments.

Please don't misunderstand me. Dedicating your life, yourself, to one other person is not easy, by any stretch of the imagination. Yet, if we walk into a marriage with a contract perspective, we choose to bound that relationship in conditional love. If the conditions are right, we stay; if the conditions are not right, we go. Truly a recipe for failure if there ever was one.

Covenant Marriage
If you want to experience love at a deeper level with your spouse, set aside unrealistic conditions to make room for love to grow. By accepting your marriage as a covenant before God, you are choosing a spiritual agreement with no legal implications. And better still, when you receive it that way, the covenant is a perpetual promise. Regardless of the situation or circumstance, a Godly covenant cannot be breached or canceled.

Covenant is not an incredibly common word these days. You may occasionally hear it in reference to certain types of agreements. However, its use within the Bible had a very special meaning. Covenant was a promise bound in blood. A do or die promise. Therefore, giving up was never an option, unless you were giving up your life.

If you spend any time reading or studying the Bible, you'll see the word 'love' used an awful lot, too. Unfortunately, love is not always the best word choice to replace the original text. According to Wikipedia, [1] there are four types of Biblical love.

The Four Loves of the Bible
- Storge – empathy bond.
- Philios – friend bond.
- Eros – romantic love.
- Agape – unconditional "God" love.

Agape love is unconditional love. Our ability to have this kind of love comes from our accepting the love of God. Because He loves us without condition, we can also love others without condition.

Only with an understanding of the life and death seriousness of a Holy Covenant, and the powerful nature of real Agape Love, can we truly begin to appreciate the power of a Marriage Covenant. While the seasons and circumstances may change in our lives, true agape love between a married couple can remain constant and consistent. Understand, though, that it truly is a daily practice. By learning and working toward healthy habits and always feeding yourself with truthful knowledge, you give yourself the tools needed to stand firm through any hard season or trial.

A covenant, especially a marriage covenant, is sacred, created with the expectation of making sacrifices. We also need to be prepared to embrace our differences as men and women, and as individuals. And above all else, we need to adopt a forgiving spirit, as we all make mistakes and fall short. As couples, we need to make sound moral agreements together and work together to stick by them. Whereas a contract can be made public, with a marriage covenant, the specifics should remain private, between both spouses and God. Your successes should be celebrated, and your failures should find forgiveness and be a source of learning.

We find ourselves living in very confusing times regarding what this world accepts, cherishes, rewards, and even what it punishes. We are told by the world what to do, how to live, and how to love. We are caught in a web of judgment and rejection, especially when we take a chance at being different. That's all that Holy really means. It means to be different, set apart. God wants us to have a Holy Matrimony, a sacred, extraordinary marriage. And it's that courage to stand out that differentiates us from the crowd. "Don't live by the contract, live by the covenant."

Your goal should be wanting to stay married, right? Why else would you decide to start a lifelong journey? A temporary marriage will get particularly complicated, especially if you have children together. Setting a proper foundation for your marriage is akin to conditioning yourself before climbing a mountain. Strengthen yourself well enough so you can commit to the goal. Be clear, and set those intentions right now, to make your marriage a lifelong commitment. Anything worth having or achieving takes preparation, training, and real effort. This means preparing yourselves both mentally and emotionally for the journey ahead.

When an ice climber decides to scale a mountain, the person doesn't simply load up the car and drive over one afternoon. There is quite a bit of preparation that must take place first. The harder the climb, the more they will need to prepare and train. Their body needs to be able to perform and endure, which means physical training. They need to know where the proper approaches are for the mountain (where to start). They'll also want to learn the various routes and likely have a primary, secondary, and even tertiary route in case of trouble.

Climbers must have necessary technical skills in order to be prepared for their trip. Their bodies must be conditioned and trained, so physical as well as mental preparation is mandatory for the challenge. Climbers train for a minimum of 16 weeks prior to the trip, employing cardio, interval workouts and extended hiking days to be ready for the trek.

Proper training conditions you to carry out your marriage commitment as well. In our marriage, one of the techniques my wife and I now practice is to pause in the middle of an argument or pray before we make a major decision. It's essential for us to be intentional with our efforts, to take a second and think things through before discussing an issue and coming to a conclusion.

If you are newlyweds or a couple thinking about getting married, here are a few questions to consider: Have you mapped out a plan for your life? Do you want kids? If so, how many? Do you want to own a home or rent? Where do you want to live? Have you decided on careers? These are common questions that I'm sure many of you have already answered. But, the key in answering these questions properly is to understand why something is important and how to remap as plans change. Kids, living environments, and the career you have or want are all intertwined.

When I decided to take my wife's hand in marriage, I calculated a lot of those questions into my plan. I knew that because Tia was in the military as a reservist, we would be taken care of medically and have a solid financial backstop. At the time, I was working part-time for an airline and positioning myself to climb the corporate ladder. I quickly discovered that my well-intended calculations were completely off; I had not taken into account the lemons that life was going to throw at us.

The first hit came when a division of the company I worked for was sold, and its structure changed dramatically. New management made the work environment very stressful. My plans to climb the ladder were thwarted so I decided to accept a demotion which resulted in even fewer hours for less pay. Shortly after that, while we were pregnant with our second daughter, Genesis, we discovered that Tia was going to be laid off from her civilian job. So now, with Tia in her third trimester and a new 12-month lease at a costly apartment in downtown Atlanta, we realized we could no longer afford to pay all of our bills. The stress of our deepening debt and inability to pay our bills was becoming unbearable, and there came a point when Tia and I seriously contemplated getting a divorce. We were worn down and could not stop arguing long enough to work together toward solutions.

It's not enough for you to know where you're going to live, how many kids you want, or even the type of careers you plan to have. You must also have an understanding of what to do if those plans fail. The best laid plans of husband and wife often go astray. You want two kids, you'll have two sets of triplets. You want a house on the beach, you end up living in a desert, or a storm washes your beach house away. You land that perfect job, only to have the company close their doors two months later. You will be tossed about like a rowboat in a hurricane, but realize that your most crucial responsibility as a couple is to learn how to anticipate problems and adapt to them so that you can strategize through them as a team!

The next Chapter will serve as an example, a breakdown of sorts, on preparing and conquering problems. It's something you can keep in mind as you are planning your future. Even if you have been married for a while, it's never too late to step back, remap and plan!

3. GEARING UP

When I was considering stories from various sources about the woes of being unprepared, an amusing but relevant one from my mountaineering friend, Mr. Charly Oliver, came to mind. I asked him if I could share it here to help paint a clear picture for my readers about the need to be adequately prepared.

"My climbing partner and I planned to climb the north face of Mt. Edith Cavell in the Canadian Rockies. We sat at the base of the north face for three days waiting for a weather window, while sorting our gear, over and over. After hours agonizing over what to put in our kit, we decided that our approach shoes, which are worn comfortably while walking for long distances, would stay behind. Although fairly light, they take up a lot of space in the pack.

On the route up, this made sense, but on the route down, we would traverse the backside of the mountain, forcing us to make the long, tedious walk all the way back around the mountain in our climbing boots. Two days and nights on the route, covering eight miles in plastic mountain boots would be grueling. When my partner and I finally reached that part of our trek, we sat in the warm sun in a beautiful grassy meadow trying to get psyched for the long walk out. Suddenly, my partner pulled his approach shoes out of his pack. He snuck them in when I wasn't looking. I never felt so betrayed in my life! He walked in comfort; I walked in agony. By the time we got back to the trailhead (1.5 miles from where we'd parked the car). My feet were hammered. I dropped my pack, took off my boots, and made my partner walk to get the car."

Charly's missing gear, his comfortable shoes, seemed at first glance to be optional. Understand that gear is extremely important for mountaineers; every item they take with them has a specific job. The lack of a critical piece, at the wrong time, could cost a mountaineer his life. Before climbing a mountain, the climber must first sit down and assess what gear is preferable based on the terrain they plan on venturing across. From what needs to be worn to the tools in their pack. And of course, it's crucial that pre-planning is made well before the ascent up a mountain.

To put it in perspective, there are many tools and attachments required when mountaineering. The gear would include, but is not limited to, a harness, ice screws, Belay devices, mountaineering boots, approach shoes, Carabiners, quickdraws, slings, and cords. Obviously, a lot of these tools are unfamiliar to many. Still, you can just as easily say they are equivalent to a lifeguard having a hip pack, life preserver, and a whistle. Or a police officer having body armor, handcuffs and a gun. It's important to be prepared with the right gear for your job or your mission.

I believe that it was the Boy Scouts who used to say, "Be Prepared." That's something that each of us needs to consider for every aspect of our life.

That helmet needed for ice climbing can also find good use in a lot of marital situations. It seemed as soon as we got married, Tia and I were repeatedly hit with all kinds of "falling ice.". You can't prevent or predict failing ice, but you can accept that it happens, be prepared for it as best you can, and deal with it when it drops on your head.

The falling ice mostly came from situations outside of our marriage that slowly crept in to cause destruction. It felt as though this falling ice was really hitting me harder as the wife. Aside from preparing for our new baby, I was contacted by detectives saying that my sister had been missing. The search continued for over a month. I was worried that something happened to her because shortly before her disappearance, she asked me to move in with me and my husband. We were in no position to take in a 17-year-old while having a 1-year-old and newborn on the way. So we declined. The Amber alerts became less hopeful and the shares on facebook began to seem like a lost cause. The day I got the news that she was found I knew at that point what the circumstance was. I was shattered. I remember screaming at the top of my lungs and my husband was my biggest supporter. He held me so tight. He prayed for me, he reminded me to rest, he reminded me to feel again. I never dealt with that grief, I just held it in and continued to go to work the next day. I just kept pushing forward out of my own strength. As we continued further, my husband vowed to make every day special for me. He always surprised me with gifts and took me on many vacations. But for me, it wasn't enough because my husband was trying to heal inside of me, what only God could heal. Eventually, the financial burden became too deep as my husband's job changed structures and I was laid off. We started arguing because we couldn't connect anymore. I started to feel hopeless when he wasn't around and was codependent on him showing up for me every day. I cared not about how he was feeling, or if he had a bad day, I just knew it felt like I was suffocating without him. We knew that it wasn't lack of love that distanced us, but the constant trials we faced. I was offered to join a support group for Grief at Victory World Church, but I was ready to face that grief. We began to argue more. It felt like it was more of a chore being in the marriage, than a fulfilling partnership. I learned to celebrate life more and the most challenging thing in my life was just another lemon life threw at us, but one that was eventually squeezed into the perfect glass of lemonade.

My family has had to deal with unexpected health scares, various financial problems, and family relationship issues. All the while, we coped with this drama while having a level of understanding between us that was not as good as it should have been. Have I mentioned yet that we have two beautiful young daughters? Children who have, on occasion, been the source of a few unforeseen issues, too. Our lives up to this point have been a challenge, worthy of the best of helmets to protect us. We've come to understand that many of our earlier issues were caused by a fundamental lack of education about marriage, and how to make it work. For example, Tia and I have come a very long way when it comes to making financial decisions. whether it be the pointless cost of items or simply unnecessary spending in general. Strange that now, we have come to a point where we laugh at the decisions we made in the past and wonder what we were thinking.

A lot of the struggles, challenges, and "falling ice" that we dealt with could have been avoided had we been adequately geared up through proper planning. It's been said that financial planning before marriage is like purchasing insurance. You hope not to need it, but you're sure glad to have it when you do. A lot of couples don't bother to invest the time, effort, and money required to deal with a possible mishap in life. In neglecting this obligation, they go about their lives under the false assumption that nothing bad will ever happen. Well, Tia and I will tell you that this is simply not true. Plan and prepare, that's your insurance.

As the saying goes, those who fail to plan actually are planning to fail. This is why we've worked very hard on things like financial literacy and have made it a crucial part of our Mountaineering Marriage life coaching course. We believe it is vital that everyone learn the essential tools to properly plan for your family's future.

> **Personal Challenge:** I challenge you to sit down with your spouse and figure out what's essential to you and your marriage. George Ellis, a noted theoretical physicist, said, "It's better to have it and not need it, than to need it and not have it."[2]

The hard truth is this: there is little that is easy when it comes to marriage. To have a truly successful and healthy one, you have to work at seeing and feeling happiness. I wish there was a lifehack I could share with you to help you avoid a lot of the challenges. It doesn't exist, so don't bother looking. Instead, make your goal to become stronger, to succeed, and then to inspire. Remember, you can't grow yourself or your marriage if you take short cuts.

4. DYNAMIC PARTNERSHIP

Ice climbers work with a partner, and within that partnership, trust is critical. A climber wants to know that their partner is proficient enough in the basics to handle the different types of situations they might encounter. At the same time, both individuals need to have a comparable and safe measure of mountain sense. When climbing, it is necessary for one of the climbers to anchor themselves and help manage the ropes while their partner continues up the mountain. This rope-enabled climbing is referred to as belaying. When you climb with a belay buddy, your partner must have the know-how and ability to operate the two main types of ropes, the dynamic and the static. While the dynamic rope serves several purposes, its crucial role is to tether the two climbers together for safety and accountability. It differs from a static rope in its ability to stretch. Unlike the static rope, the dynamic rope helps absorb the impact of a fall, as the sudden jolt caused by an unforgiving rope would be disastrous for the climber.

In rare instances when a climber has fallen into an ice crevasse or lost their hold or footing and slipped, the partner on the other end of that rope was able to recover their buddy because they were tethered together. In ice climbing, a knowledgeable partner isn't just useful, they're mandatory.

So it goes with life. You need someone you can trust tied to you, someone who will have your back in case of an emergency, or who gives you peace of mind simply from knowing there's someone on the other end of the rope. In our relationships, sometimes we need the static rope and sometimes we need the dynamic rope. There are times we need to be held fast and times that we need to be able to stretch a little. At all times, we need someone we can trust who will gently catch us before we fall.

As I've mentioned before, my wife, Tia, is an active duty military member. The girls and I could not be more proud of all that she has accomplished, as she works with her team to help keep our great nation safe. However, life as a service member is never an easy one. A military job can be uniquely stressful. You are literally dealing with life and death consequences for the decisions and actions of yourself and those around you. But no matter what anxiety Tia has to deal with, she can trust that she has an anchor in me. She knows that I will always be here for her, to assure her and affirm her, and to bring her back to a calm state of mind. And likewise, as my trusted partner, Tia supports my aspirations and goals, and she helps to hold me accountable as well.

I sometimes have to remind Donnell of his divine calling in life. He knows that he is talented but often doubts himself. He wonders if he is good enough and if he'll succeed. I mean, he wrote this amazing book because he truly wants to inspire marriages. The point of a dynamic partnership is to explore gifts and talents together and to push one another toward greatness. I listen to all of the songs that he writes. I critique them and I enjoy them. I give him someone he can look to for encouragement and

honesty. We coach each other and we cheer each other on. We dynamically provide for each other what we know we will need in return.

I mentioned that during our financial hail storm, I had decided to give up my leadership position at the airline company. I could feel that their changes in management, along with the new policies, were stressing me out. I was overburdened by work, unappreciated by my bosses, and underpaid for my efforts. It was a hard choice to make, to step back from more authority and responsibility, and to take a reduction in pay. The person on the other end of my rope – Tia – served as my lifeline when she reminded me of my goals and that I hadn't desired a long-term career with this company anyway. Her understanding, knowledge, and support encouraged me so that I could make the right decisions for our future. In partnering with Tia, I set myself an anchor of accountability, with that, she has always kept me focused on my goals.

Being able to submit to your partner in this way is not easy. It involves being utterly humble, setting aside your pride. You need to respectfully share each of your concerns, divulge your most private thoughts. But if you genuinely feel that you cannot discuss something with your spouse, you may need to share those concerns with a counselor. Human beings are wonderfully complicated beings, but we don't always have it together. However, you can maintain open communications with your spouse, as they will ultimately know you better than anyone else in this world.

Poor Tia! I tell her everything that goes through my head – and that's a lot of information! My poor wife goes on a far-reaching mental journey with me, daily. She knows that my purpose and calling are well-rooted inside me. It's truly a message that I believe I need to share with the world. Because I have made my wife a part of my purpose, should I pass away before my mission is complete, I can trust that Tia will be able to continue with the work of spreading my message. We've established our marriage as a healthy and sound one, and she knows how to help fulfill my purpose because she truly understands me as a person, as I know her. I want our kids to learn who their earthly father is as well as their Heavenly one. I want them to know all about my challenges as well as my accomplishments. This is a scary truth, but it is the truth; your marriage is both your legacy and your empire.

There are common misconceptions regarding openness and sub-missiveness in a marriage. One of the hardest mountains I've had to climb in marriage is that mountain called pride. Looking back, this was the mountain that ruined my first marriage. I didn't have the right gear or critical knowledge. I listened to people who acted as guides but sent me on all the wrong paths. Being totally unprepared caused me and my ex-wife to fall, with no dynamic rope to catch us, and ultimately, we were unable to recover. Today, with the experience I gained through trial and error, as well as more deliberate research, I developed a new viewpoint. I will share that viewpoint now to help you better understand the proper roles in a submissive marriage.

Before we go down this road, I'd like for you to ponder this question: who do you think "wears the pants" in a marriage? Is it the person who makes more money? Does the smartest one always get to lead or is it solely just the fact of being a man that gives you all the authority? A lot of couples struggle to answer these simple questions. Your current viewpoint or bias will color your answer. You might answer one way in front of your partner or spouse, but feel the opposite to be true.

Confession time. Back when I was dating, I was often picked on by my friends and coworkers for not "putting my foot down" with the women I dated. They proclaimed, quite forcefully, that I didn't understand my position or authority as a man. After I got married, I was continually told by those same "friends" that a man needed to "crack the whip" on his wife, demanding respect. So, I tried it in my first marriage. Unfortunately, it wasn't until the marriage had ended that I realized this was horrible advice.

If you allow it, everybody and their mother will find a way to inject their own two cents about how you should run your marriage. But your marriage is between you and your spouse; you have full control over how your home should be run. Your spouse and God are the only ones who should have a say in how your marriage operates. If you are a man and want to let your wife take the role as the leader of your finances, don't let anyone outside your marriage guilt you into something different. Take pride in dividing roles that complement each other's strengths, not societal normalities. Conversely, if as the man, you want to be the leader in the marriage, then you need to understand that there is a right way to go about it.

In my marriage to Tia, I work hard to earn her respect. Not just by being a man, but by putting in the effort to educate myself on what it takes to be a leader. In our house, I strive to be the educator, the healer, the counselor, and the protector. Since my wife had a more traditional career in the military, I strived to be the nurturer for our children when she was not around, You could have called me Mr. Mom. This means I cooked, did hair, washed clothes, etc. These are all things that, for generations, society has said that the wife is supposed to do. But I did them all with a smile on my face. Why? Because I embrace the joy in leading and protecting my family.

Sometimes, roles reverse and I will gladly take on jobs that a woman would traditionally do. When I wasn't working, I made sure my wife had lunch to eat at work; I prepared dinner at home for our family. While I wasn't perfectly consistent, I accepted that I had to do whatever it took for the progression of this family. Marriage works because both partners bring something to the table.

Donnell was truly my rock in times when I felt like I needed one, but in return, I made sure that I laid things out as smoothly as possible. I would make sure that the kid's clothes were organized and easily obtainable. I would suggest meals or order food to the home if they needed it. We worked together constantly even when situations were not ideal. He always made sure that I had gifts when I came home from an extended absence, and I also made sure to think of nice gestures to show my appreciation. I rented a pontoon boat for his birthday one year and to see his smile made the world of a difference. Ultimately, it's not about the individual roles we perform that make us successful at marriage, but about the unity, we practice as we adapt to different scenarios.

There was this incident a while back when Tia had a flat tire that needed to be changed. As I worked on it, I had a hard time getting the lug nuts off. Tia happened to recall that hair spray works as a lubricant when lugs nuts are on too tight. Voila! It worked. A friend of mine teased me about this incident, but I didn't mind. I prayed that God give me a strong woman as my mate, and He did just that.

Is a man emasculated for taking on non-traditional roles in his home? Absolutely not. I always tell Tia, an opinion is only what you believe to be true, it's not necessarily the truth. This is our world, our marriage; we choose whom we invite into our circle. Another person's opinion need not be heard unless asked for, and even then, it holds little value compared to our own. Thus far, this strategy has worked for us. When I submitted to the idea of having a humbled heart, I stopped battling the insecurities and listening to others' voices; instead, I focused my energy toward finding the real purpose that God wanted for my marriage. In my search for that purpose, God revealed his gracious gifts within Tia and me. Now we are in a position to use those gifts to help others in their marriages.

I take great pride in my marriage, knowing that our time and effort have created a strong partnership. But we didn't start out this way. In the beginning, we bumped heads and could not seem to get along. There were times that I felt the marriage wasn't working out; I convinced myself that throwing in the towel had to be an option. In fact, Tia and I separated twice and didn't know if it was going to work between us.

Consider This: What do you think happens when one or both climbers decide to release the ropes from their harness?

When you sit comfortably in your own soft, cozy chair at home, it's easy to feel safe and allow your connection to slip. But change the terrain to one that is blanketed in snow, covered in a treacherous layer of thin ice, and you would think twice before abandoning your partner. At any moment, you could step in the wrong place, fall into a well-hidden crevasse, and without that tether to your partner, you'd fall all the way down. At all times, whether in a cozy setting or on treacherous ice, you need to stay connected in a stable and meaningful way to your partner. They can help to catch you and hold you back from going somewhere you don't really want to go.

The consequences of leaving my family seem unfathomable now. How could I possibly walk away, knowing that I'm their protector? What would that do to my wife, a person I have grown to love more than myself? Sure, I suppose that eventually my wife would find a way to heal and ultimately be okay. But divorce can irreparably damage any person, both mentally and physically, and have long-lasting effects on others around you in ways you could never anticipate.

How do we ensure that our marriages don't cause this kind of suffering? Create a dynamic and robust partnership. To do that, we need to understand what a healthy relationship actually looks like. We start with two unique people with two drastically different personalities (or three, according to my wife, since I'm a Gemini) that settle into three distinct relationship categories: Codependence, Independence, and Interdependence. Each relationship has its own characteristics. But in the end, there's only one that works best for a healthy marriage.

Codependent Relationship

Relationships are complicated. No two ways about it. When you encounter another person, bring them into your circle, and spend time with them, there are going to be good times and bad times. We all come to relationships with our own specific needs and desires, and when we add another person to that equation, it's difficult to get all those needs and desires met.

In the relationship category, Codependence is a difficult one. Clinically speaking, a codependent relationship occurs when one partner attaches their happiness and identity to the fulfillment of another. Most often, the type of person they connect with is one who could care less about their partner's needs or desires, only their own. It's a textbook example of opposites attracting. And while it can come in various degrees of imbalance, this relationship usually ends with one partner abusing the other, physically or mentally.

I believe most people are good and that most truly want what's best for their partner, for that spouse to be happy. But we struggle to know them as well as we could or should, and to know how to meet their needs. Simply put, we don't know - how to get them to that place called happy. What drives our desire to make our partners happy? Love. And to understand what love truly means, go back to where it all started. The Bible has an excellent prescription of love.

Scripture Reading: 1 Corinthians 13:4-8
4. Love is patient, love is kind. It does not envy, it does not boast, it is not proud. **5.** It does not dishonor others, it is not self-seeking, it is not easily angered, it keeps no record of wrongs. **6.** Love does not delight in evil but rejoices with the truth. **7.** It always protects, always trusts, always hopes, always perseveres. **8.** Love never fails. But where there are prophecies, they will cease; where there are tongues, they will be stilled; where there is knowledge, it will pass away.

Now, compare the nature of a codependent relationship to this type of love; they are not aligned at all. One person tries to please the other, to make themselves happy. And the other person takes advantage of that behavior. This is a very dangerous relationship, and if we start behaving this way, we must put a stop to this destructive behavior. I fear that a lot more people these days have a marriage that resembles a Codependent Relationship, yet they are unaware of this. My previous marriage may have fallen victim to this.

Codependency can be mistaken for love. But look back at our scripture, 1 Corinthians 13:4-8. Here you find a description of healthy love. If this does not reflect your own relationship, then I urge you to reevaluate.

In a Codependent relationship, the dependent partner perceives themselves and their needs based on their partner, creating an excessive reliance. Their reasons for needing this person are unhealthy, and while each person may feel their partner is the solution to their problems, that's never true. Codependents are drawn to one another, but when they are together, the results are disastrous at best. Of course, there are degrees of codependent relationships, but hopefully this gives you insight, and if this is your situation, I believe that there is still hope. Behaviors are the results of decisions, and decisions the result of a worldview or mindset. I am going to give you the tools to expand your worldview.

Independent Relationship

Everyone knows what it means to be independent; that is, unless you're 40 years old and have never moved out of your parent's home. Personal independence is a good thing. But can it be too much of a good thing? Possibly, if it negatively affects your relationship.

Things to consider: What is healthy independence in a relationship? How can one recognize excessive independent tendencies when it comes to their relationship? Is it even possible to be independent and have a healthy relationship?

People who have excessive independent tendencies almost expect their relationship to run on autopilot. But relationships require real work. Daily. If you are only doing what it takes to improve and develop yourself, you cannot expect your relationship to progress.. Consistent and sufficient work must be done in order to grow in your relationship with your spouse. One example is open communication, which is often nearly non-existent in an excessively independent relationship.

A friend once told me that the type of person you are when you are single will only be amplified when you are married. That's because you will seek and notice a reflection of yourself in your spouse. If you were a completely independent single person, you have to work extra hard to apply positive principles in your marriage. Some independent people don't want to get married at all; they aren't as afraid of commitment as they are fearful of giving up their sense of control. But if you decide to commit to bonding your life with another person, you will need to be aware of the type of habits you have developed so you can correct them

I once asked a married friend what happiness and success meant to them. The answer was simply, "Having more money and a bigger house." When I asked her the follow-up question, when is enough, enough, her answer was, "It will never be enough." There are some critical takeaways from this exchange. Aside from the lack of an actual attainable goal of fulfillment, notice how they didn't mention anything about their spouse? Textbook independent relationship mentality. Chances are, this person's happiness ideal was developed before marriage. She was likely always driven and independent. But when you choose to get married, you need to change your focus and priority to include more than your own achievements and desires. It is assuredly hard to recover from this way of self-centered thinking, yet changing this perspective and mindset is still very possible and will result in a healthier relationship.

Interdependent Relationship

Have you ever watched someone spin a plate on a stick, walk a tightrope, or hang off the side of a mountain from just their fingertips? In each case, the performer will tell you that when it comes to accomplishing those feats, balance is everything. The same can be said for healthy relationships.

An Interdependent relationship thrives on balance and it is the best kind to foster for a healthy marriage. Both partners develop a natural give and take, based upon a mutual desire to sustain and grow their relationship. Not by magic; by choice. They make a purposeful set of conscious decisions, brought about by an intention to build a better marriage. First, you have to want it, then you have to learn how to do it, and then you do it!

It seemed like it took a long time for my wife and me to get to this point in our marriage. We had more than our fair share of differences at the start! For one, Tia was a very independent person and brought that with her to the relationship. Between being in the military and living as a single mom, she had totally adapted to the idea that she'd have to do things for herself. I saw this independence right from the start when we were dating. Tia would carry her six-month-old daughter, Ava, in the car seat, along with her diaper bag, and all of Tia's own things, never once asking for help. It never occurred to her that when you have a partner, you can work together to lighten the load on yourself and share duties with each other. I was raised as a gentleman and one of my biggest pet peeves was that Tia would just walk up and open doors for herself. Oftentimes, she would be ahead of me and I had to rush forward if I didn't want her to open a door herself. We had to communicate about needs and desires and shared responsibilities, but now Tia graciously allows me to open doors for her. The idea of marriage is rooted in symbolism and Tia and I understand that there are vital roles a husband or wife embrace to cement a shared vision of a healthy marriage.

As a musician, I picture an interdependent relationship as an orchestra, with all three characteristics creating a beautiful balance. Each musician practices individually, by themselves, with the common goal of joining with the others to perform the same musical score. Each musician must lean on another to complement the sounds, while at the same time not overbearing each other. When the sounds of all the musicians intertwine, they work together to create a balance of melodies.

There is nothing wrong with being dependent on your spouse. This is what God intended for us, as husband and wife, to become one flesh. First, we must learn some fundamental principles about balance if we are to have a healthy relationship and marriage. One key principle: we do not own our partners. They are their own independent people, with individual needs and desires. We can be a team without losing all of ourselves. For that to work, we must first have self-love. That's a critical piece because if we do not love ourselves, we will try to fill an emotional void from external sources. Next, we must work on ourselves daily through prayer and meditation. As we get a firmer grip on our own sense of self, we can join our spouse with a humble and loving heart to create balance – our symphony.

Tia and I have become living examples of this balance. We lean on each other daily but know how to self-improve as well, bettering the relations of our marriage. In this balance, where I am weak, she is strong. When she slips or falls, I am there to pick her up. When I find myself lost, she helps me regain my way through wisdom. You must secure that rope with your partner, and never let go. Trust your partner to have your back.

Speaking directly to the men, make sure you protect and feed your wife with knowledge, yet also give her room to bloom. Give her the power to protect you, as well, because we are not invincible to either the physical or spiritual world.

For the women, you are that natural nurturer, so please work to have patience with your husband. Often, it takes time for a man to assume the king's role in a marriage. Your husband will need your help. So, build him up both verbally and behind the scenes through prayer.

You can make it work. First, each partner needs to recognize that they have duties as you both climb the mountain of your marriage. You both need to learn how to properly fulfill those duties and equip yourselves with the right gear. Then, you need to start the climb and do the work to live out those roles in love as defined in the Bible. If you follow these critical steps, I sincerely believe you will produce a dynamic partnership.

5. THE CLIMB

Had I known better, I would have done a lot of things differently with Tia. I try not to look back with regret at my past, but rather to be grateful for my journey. I am content with the life that I have here and now. Yet, everything I have learned and accomplished would be in vain if I didn't utilize life's invaluable lessons to not only build a stronger marriage for myself, but also to use my experience and knowledge to help others. We only know what we know, until we learn something new. We must constantly search for answers and deeper understanding so that we can grow. Marriages require preparation and hard work. From creating good habits to protecting yourself from seen and unseen forces, you need a well-crafted plan to get it done right. If you properly train your mind to become aware of both the mental and spiritual battles ahead, then you will have a greater chance to prevail when faced with undesired trials.

"The climb" is an everyday challenge in marriage; it's constant. There are always new battles to fight and serious problems to fix. Battles within ourselves and challenges with our partner. A happy marriage doesn't come easily, but there are major factors that play a role in your ability to overcome specific challenges in your partnership.

One essential element for a healthy marriage is physical health. That surprises most people. I am not a nutritionist, but I have discovered that eating right and some level of exercise plays a huge role in a thriving marriage. For a mountain climber, nutrition is obviously crucial. Climbers must eat the right foods in the right amount in order to have the energy to endure the climb. Trainers warn that a climber's body will experience postprandial somnolence, aka food coma, a drowsy and fatigue state, from overeating the wrong things. To a lesser degree, our daily nutrition and exercise will affect the climb we experience with our marriage as well. We'll share more about building a healthy lifestyle plan for your family as part of future Mountaineer Marriage courses.

In my own journey toward better fitness, I learned that my body does not break down beef or pork very well. After I had taken a break from eating those meats, I started eating them again and became fatigued, falling asleep in the middle of the day and hitting the pillow at night completely drained. My energy levels dropped, I stopped going to the gym regularly, and I gained weight. Tia experienced this as well. It's hard to maintain a healthy marriage when you are both exhausted and unwell. But once you fall off the healthy living path, it isn't easy to get back on. So, how do you do that? Tia and I had to set realistic and achievable goals for ourselves, change our mindset, and fortify our will power. It worked and we're back to healthy living so you'll want to consider creating a healthy diet plan for you and your family.

Investing in your health will also invest in your marriage. When you exercise with your partner, you spend quality time together and gain a partner who holds you accountable. You bond over a shared interest in each other's physical fitness, and that will lead to a generally happier and more sexual marriage. In addition to the gym time Tia and I share, we each have our own fitness favorites. She works with a personal trainer, and I practice Jiu Jitsu, a fun sport that is also a great form of fitness training. Whatever your choice, if you can create this healthy habit in your relationship, you are on your way to becoming a true power couple.

When planning for the long climb of a Mountaineer Marriage, you need to condition yourself both mentally and physically to better prepare for your family's future. Fortunately, you are never on this climb alone. You will likely come across fellow climbers who are going the same direction as you. These "fellow climbers," aka other married couples, should be considered your marriage community. It's not always easy to find other couples going the same direction as you nor is it easy to find the time to connect with them. Understandably, each couple is busy focusing on their family but it's important to make time to involve yourself with other couples.

Connect with folks who are relatable, and at a similar or higher level on their marriage climb. If you are part of a church, find a small marriage group. If you are not part of a church, or your church does not provide things like this, try certain social websites like meetup.com. If you are still having trouble finding a marriage community after checking exhausting those resources, then celebrate your good fortune in finding the "Mountaineer Marriage Community"! We would love for everyone to become a part of all that we provide!

Keep Your Trash With You
Climbing etiquette says, pack it in, pack it out. And when it comes to marriage and social media, where you put 'your trash' is equally important. I know couples who are going through extreme battles in their marriage. How do I know about their personal business? Because their trash is constantly being dumped on social media! I see good, well-meaning couples dump all their issues and problems on sites like Facebook, creating somewhat of a dependence on the response of others. Exposing your personal issues to others may temporarily suppress how you feel, but it

does nothing to actually fix your problems. Trust me, not every one of those "friends" on your list wishes the best for you and your marriage. We all tend to feed off both good and bad energy, so make sure you are intentional with your actions.

When two couples are relatable, there is a sense of sincere compassion. People who go through the same issue as you are more willing to help you if you need it. When you share your struggles with people you know and trust - versus anonymous people on the Internet - you have more control over who knows your personal business.

Initially, my wife and I spent a lot of time alone with no marriage community. During that time, we dealt with our problems through anger and confusion. Thankfully, we were able to learn the ropes and overcome our issues, but having another couple to lean on at those critical points of our climb would have made our lives so much better and gotten us through our issues with less effort and struggle. So, let's be mindful of where we dump our trash and find the right people to trust. The more we avoid exposing marital problems to the world via the Internet, the better off we will be.

Embrace Nature

When I go walking or hiking, I rarely listen to music. I've learned to enjoy hearing my footsteps on the ground, listening to the birds, taking notice of the wind blowing through the trees, and getting the chance to smell and breathe fresh air. I take in nature fully, being grateful for all of my senses. Our brain constantly collects memories through our experiences, and I don't want to miss out on anything. Unfortunately, with the bombardment of new technology, popular streaming shows, and a jam-packed calendar of events, we often forget to enjoy the little things.

One day, Tia came home and was surprised to see our living room had completely changed. I had taken the TV out and replaced it with a bookshelf. I had placed pillows and a rug on the floor, along with a small lamp. I had soothing music playing. I had created a meditative environment by eliminating distractions. Since that day, my wife has grown to love this new decor because this change has had a positive, calming aspect on our lives.

Through their daily practices, monks embody this peaceful meditation and mindfulness. As I studied their ways, I started teaching my daughters to eat and enjoy their meals without the distractions of their tablets and TV. I have encouraged my family to become more present in the moment, instead of being unconscious to the real world around us. As a result, we have learned to focus more and get more done each day. Tia and I now view our life together differently; we aren't caught up in our phones or recording every moment of our life. We are present in the moment, living our life fully. I encourage you to do the same.

You can still enjoy technology, don't get me wrong. However, when Tia and I decided to virtually eliminate distractions in our life, we noticed the profound positive effect it had on our marriage. Back when Tia and I lived in downtown Atlanta, I played a lot of video games. I was working part-time, intending to use my free time to work on my music. But whenever I was at home, I would hop on the video game console and play it for hours! It didn't seem to bother Tia, but at the same time, I got absolutely nothing done. I disconnected from reality and lived in autopilot. To this day, I don't know how I lived like that. On very rare occasions, Tia and I will still play a little competitive "Call of Duty" on our mobile phones, but we have shifted our priorities in life and have become very conscious of how we spend our time.

The Frostbite

Mountaineer marriage compares marriage to the act of climbing an ice mountain. I chose this analogy because I believe that there are relatable scenarios and situations between the two. The terrain of an icy mountain is much more unpredictable than that of a stone mountain. The slick, icy slopes necessitate that you are highly aware of your surroundings, moving forward in a slow, deliberate and careful manner. One wrong step can be life-threatening in an environment that can be well below 0 degrees.

Have you ever had frostbite? If so, you know that it can be very painful and recovery can be a slow process; sometimes, recovery is not possible at all. Oddly, when your bodily tissues freeze, you experience numbness, followed by severe pain. In your marriage, there will be times when you are in a rut, so conditioned to your everyday patterns that you can develop a "frostbite" state of mind. Every day looks the same, and a cooling of your relationship can occur. This "cooling" causes you to become numb to your spouse. How does this manifest in a marriage? Lack of conversation, no more date nights, repeatedly arguing over the same issues. Does that sound eerily familiar?

At times during our marriage, Tia and I have suffered through this same condition. We got caught up in our work or busy schedules, and we shifted to autopilot and began to neglect each other. This not only affected my marriage, it hurt my relationship with my two little girls. Tia would ask if I wanted to go out, and I would come up with excuses, find a way to refuse. This became a source of several arguments within our home. "You never spend time with me and the girls." "You're always sitting in front of that computer." Or the most difficult to hear, "When are you coming home?" The sound of frustration in, "You don't communicate with me anymore" and, "You need to spend time with the girls." It seemed like there were never enough hours in my day nor did I know how to divide *my* time between work, wife, and the girls.

My breakthrough came when I had to accept that I was earning those remarks. I needed to do better. So, I sat down and created a schedule for myself. I could no longer continue to neglect my responsibility as a father to my girls, nor as a husband to my wife.

Deep down, I knew that if I continued to stay in that numb state in my marriage with this "frostbite" mentality, then I would establish a damaging pattern from which it would be harder to break. This was my experience; if the way you live your life works for you and your spouse, then as I've said before, don't let me or anyone tell you otherwise. However, if you are looking for a way to grow your relationship, and you and your spouse have a vision for a greater purpose, then sit down and create a plan to help manage your time so you don't suffer from marital frostbite.

Falling Debris And Avalanches

My interviews with multiple ice climbers revealed climbing situations that are simply unavoidable. Falling ice debris is one of those concerns. Ice climbers are bound to get hit in the head, as the mountain is constantly shifting, moving, and melting. This is why helmets are so important. If the ice falls from high distances, you could be seriously injured or die. Another inescapable danger is an avalanche. While a helmet can protect you from falling ice, nothing can protect you from an avalanche that can bury you in snow and potentially kill you.

So, what exactly is a marital avalanche? Here's the tricky part: it's not simply one thing. It's a consortium of dangerous situations that you allow into your marriage, and those situations can bury it.

As you may already know, Tia and I have a weekly marriage podcast. We have an episode called "Roots of a Healthy Marriage". In this segment, we talk about certain external aspects that can impact a marriage. We discuss divorce caused by differences over religion, about having or raising children, or about dealing with finances. I recommend that you listen to our podcast, and in particular, that episode. Here, I will dive deeper into this subject matter.

In my own marriage, we have been hit with each of these issues, along with several more, and still, we have overcome. In our home, we believe in God's Word, through Jesus Christ, whom we accept as our Lord and Savior. We understand and believe that our strength comes from the most high, and that without His guidance, we would be lost. I will openly tell anyone who comes to us that in order to have a strong marriage, you need to put the Father in the center of it. Regardless of what you believe in, in my own personal experience, having an anchor to a higher power, one who is far more powerful than ourselves, is the only way to find peace and happiness. We are all deeply flawed individuals, and to think that we can handle our problems on our own is unrealistic and erroneous. If everything seems to be getting out of control in your life, I encourage you to consider opening your heart up to God for direction. My wife and I are available if you need help or guidance toward this way of life. We provide spiritual guidance as part of our personal and marriage coaching. A healthy spiritual life is extremely important because in its essence, marriage is a spiritual act.

Before you read this next section, let me say that children are a blessing. They can also be falling debris. While our children are our priority, they should never come between you and your partner. But you must learn how to avoid that occurrence. In order to run your home in a healthy fashion, both leaders must be on the same page. Your children are always watching you, and everything you do or decide affects them. As they grow and develop, it may seem easy to elevate them above your spouse, but ultimately, they are not the ones responsible if your marriage fails. Taking responsibility for our marriage calls for a tight knit understanding of structure in the home. A child also needs to grow up understanding that when it comes to mommy and daddy, they are one and the same. Children are smart! They'll even try to put one parent against the other, so be prepared and put your heads together, so that the kids cannot pull you apart.

Finances are another form of falling debris, maybe even an avalanche. The value of a dollar has taken a considerable dive throughout the years. I can barely remember when there was a "Dollar Menu" at fast food restaurants. While we all have financial needs, we often think we need things that we don't. When I was in Rio a few years ago, I told a friend of mine that there was something peaceful about walking everywhere and not needing to have a car. Whereas back home in the U.S., I got in my car to go down the block; in Rio, it was more natural to walk. She explained to me that they viewed Americans as running in a rat race, always trying to have the next big thing. Our consumption and greed may not be totally our own fault. We have allowed ourselves to be caught up in almost hypnotic control through mass media and marketing. This is one reason it was so important for my family to get rid of our TV and instead create a better meditative environment.

By stepping away from being controlled by "distractions," we form the groundwork to make conscious financial decisions, take initiative in learning about money, and becoming financially literate. On our website (www.mountaineermarriage.com), we delve more deeply into how to better handle your finances and teach you what money is and what it truly represents. For now, however, it's sufficient for you to understand that finances will play a considerable role in your marriage. Financial troubles, like most martial issues, can be easy enough to solve and should never be used as an excuse for divorce.

In Chapter 4, The Dynamic Partnership, I cautioned that nothing or no one should come between you and your partner. If you are a man and your wife is the breadwinner, you should not feel ashamed or embarrassed. Spouses should always strive to complement each other, not compete against each other. Where your spouse is weak, you should be strong. When my wife worked and

I stayed at home, the progression of our family required me to ensure that our house was together. Even while I was out looking for a new job, I could not neglect household chores no matter if this situation was short or long term. The best partnerships comprehend that the money between you cannot be stamped with your name. All money comes in as equally shared to meet the needs of the family.

As we climb "Marriage Mountain", we must watch out for those outside forces that will come against us. Money, children, friends and even family members can come between you and your spouse. No matter how well-meaning, everyone is not on the same journey as you. Today, marriages are failing and falling way down, in great numbers. Even I find it hard sometimes to keep going when it seems that everyone around me is giving up. But remember that this is a spiritual battle and it's bigger than we think. Ask any successful person and they will tell you they did not leave their success up to chance. Their success arose from a conscious effort to excel. People fall into divorce for reasons that are not always clear. In order to successfully climb the marriage mountain, we have to deal with our inner selves and find true happiness, learn about the kinds of marital debris and avalanches which can and will come at you, and be prepared for the fight. The best advice I can offer anyone is to learn yourself, first. In the end, when you first facilitate an understanding and acceptance of who you are, you are helping yourself more than any counselor or personal coach in the world.

6. STAY ON ROUTE

An essential concept of marriage is understanding boundaries. There are numerous false proclamations and opinions spread everywhere on this subject, but I make it my personal mission to dispel those. As I've mentioned in previous chapters, if your marriage is working, no one should inject their opinion into your relationship. If it's not broke, don't fix it. However, if you desire to develop your marriage, then you need to find a legitimate way to find assistance.

Tia and I believe we have developed an approach that is both Biblically accurate and truly healthy.
One of my favorite TV commentators is Trevor Noah, the comedic host of The Daily Show. At one point, he made a statement that he is not opposed to getting married but he doesn't believe in actually living with your spouse. He explains that one of the primary reasons couples get divorced is their belief in how cohabiting relationships are supposed to work. In his opinion, it's difficult to believe that everyone was designed to live together in the same manner, especially when intimacy can be expressed in myriad ways. If this way of living truly works for him, then I will not argue the point. Maybe he was joking, but for argument's sake, let's assume that this is his honest opinion and if so, there are a lot

of potential problems with this philosophy.

If we look at the standpoint of a non-believer, this approach to seeking pleasure above purpose makes sense. However, as a believer in an all-knowing God, we must understand that His rules and instructions are meant to provide us with a better pathway. It's essential that you know that your home as a married couple is sacred; it is God's plan that you have dominion over how you run it. But for you to be effective, it needs to be run well. That means that you and your spouse get to choose how you want to run your home, and what ideas, people, practices, and things you allow to pass through your doors. You have both the right and the responsibility to create meaningful values for your family and to filter out any of the nonsense that would tear down what you have built. You and your spouse should strive to remain on the same page so that you can grow together instead of apart. It's also crucial that you create the kind of powerful family rituals that can strengthen your family today and for generations to come.

The positive aspects of a married couple living together are innumerable. So are the problems of that couple living apart, both physically and emotionally. Lack of boundaries is first on the list.

Scripture reading: Genesis 2:24
> **24.** *Therefore a man shall leave his father and his mother and hold fast to his wife, and they shall become one flesh.*

In the passage from Genesis 2:24, God is saying that a married couple becomes one. One flesh, it says. While becoming one flesh implies the physical component, this language also refers to a spiritual oneness, and both must be a constant pursuit. You obviously cannot be of one flesh when apart. This type of physical separation makes it far too easy for the devil, our enemy, to confuse the minds of a married couple.

Shortly after I announced Tia and I were engaged, my friend advised me that I needed to make my relationship known publicly by posting pictures of Tia and myself together, on our social media accounts. I didn't really understand why this mattered, until much later. Now, I wholeheartedly agree with this statement. Your Instagram or Facebook accounts should reflect that you are in a committed relationship, for all the world to see. Having a presence on social media can be akin to living in a form of virtual reality. In order to stay faithful and committed to your partner, you must avoid and reject any possible entanglement in a virtual relationship with another person.

What constitutes a virtual relationship? It's complicated. Frequently, this relationship can go unnoticed or even seem entirely harmless to those involved. If your social media persona does not reflect that you're 100% committed to your spouse, then you may invite others to connect with you, even if only online. A relationship with someone who is not your spouse, even if there is no physical interaction, can be considered cheating. In fact, there are many different forms of cheating. If you lean on someone who is not your spouse financially or emotionally, you are crossing outside the boundaries of marriage. I am friends with married people in the entertainment industry who are naturally on social media, and yet whenever I visit their profile, I do not see a single picture of their spouse, or a couples photo, on their pages. People with business-focused pages may be reluctant to share this personal information. However, if you are flaunting your body or dropping flirtatious private messages to another person on social media, you're opening the door for an attack on your marriage. At the end of the day, no one is going to care about your marriage as much as you do. The person on the other end of the DM (direct message) does not care if your spouse is devastated by the revealing picture that they send you. Or if your children end up emotionally scarred by a separation or divorce. Those are things that you and your spouse should care about and avoid at all costs.

Our society continually blurs the lines of morality by using the influencing power of the media. They create near-subliminal messages through their content and intentionally confuse the audience, especially the younger generation, about marriage. From open marriages to polyamorous relationships, the moral bar drifts lower and lower. I fear the idea of monogamist marriage will cease to exist if we continue to accept the way our culture pushes the boundaries. When I was confused about what I wanted for my marriage, I introduced the idea of an open marriage to my wife, hoping to spice things up. Although my wife disagreed, I thank God that I found my purpose for my marriage and decided to turn away from that mindset. I realize now that this type of behavior and attitude would have opened our home up to all sorts of negative energy and manufactured the opposite effect. It likely would have destroyed our marriage.

Seeing Donnell in this state, confirmed in me that he was only desperate to figure out a solution to our problem. He had to struggle with the idea of pleasing God by remaining in marriage but also feeling secure and happy in our marriage. I knew that I had to stay on the original route we were on because eventually, we would get to the top of the mountain. I had to be his anchor and not his aggressor. I listened to his heart and not his words because his heart was saying he just wanted to feel loved. Staying on route helped us both realize that we were meant to be together. We now realize there's beauty in stopping in a garden of flowers knowing that you could pick every single one, but continue walking toward our destiny with each other being the

only flower we need. We just have to water it!

Past generations of marriages don't have to battle with the same things we millennials struggle with today. They dealt with temptations, nonetheless. The enemy will always use what's available to distract, misinform, and misdirect. Today, information and social influence are far more accessible and prevalent than ever before. If you aren't mindful of what's going on, you could find yourself in a very tough situation. Don't allow yourself to fall into a virtual reality trap. There are no restart buttons in the real world. We can't choose to be committed to our spouse in the real world and to allow ourselves to "stray" in the virtual one. I would strongly encourage you to sit down and discuss this with your spouse. Both partners need to understand the dangers and determine if each of you have sufficiently healthy boundaries regarding social media. It is very easy to lose track of the seemingly innocent decisions you make in a virtual reality; in actual reality, you are harming your real marriage.

What do you do if you believe social media is causing friction with your spouse? That's easy. Shut it down! Shut it all down: Facebook, Instagram, Twitter, TikTok, and especially Snapchat. If you allow these social platforms to invade your marriage and cause arguments, cut it off cold turkey. These social media tools can drive a wedge between you and your spouse, perhaps irreparably damaging your bond. If you are in your twenties or thirties, the thought of shutting down social media probably sounds extreme, absurd, and nearly impossible. But it can be done and while painful at first, it feels freeing in the long run. Tia and I were able to completely detach ourselves from the stronghold of social media. We now live an absolutely amazing life without our emotional states being dictated by social media. I'm not saying those applications are all bad. But there's a cost that must be carefully weighed. If social media comes between you and your spouse, the cost is too high.

Maybe you're not dealing with a virtual battle. Perhaps, it's the physical world that tries to cross the boundaries of your marriage. Friends, family, and yes, parents, are all common challenges to your marriage. Tia and I have dealt with those who force their opinions on us; how we should run our marriage, raise our kids, etc. We have finally closed the borders to everyone outside our marriage except professional counselors. If someone doesn't respect your boundaries, then it's essential to close the circle, isolating yourselves from that negative energy, until respect can be reestablished.

By now, you realize that I have strong beliefs about marriage; some might say, assertive or even aggressive. Perhaps. My goal is to help marriages stay strong, and couples stay together and find happiness. No relationship is ever 100% perfect. We are all humans, striving to learn better, making mistakes along the way. It's better for your family to make sure you don't have to deal with any more drama than necessary. God forbid your marriage falters or fails; you'll find most of your friends and family will likely support your divorce instead of attempting to give positive and helpful advice.

Boundaries in a marriage are like the boundaries of a well-worn trail up a mountain. You can see that it is a tried and trusted path, one that can guide you toward your goal. Stay on the right route while heading up Marriage Mountain! I know from my own journey - and the journeys of others - that if you stray off the main path, crossing outside of those clear boundaries, you can get lost. Once you travel outside of the boundaries that you and your spouse have constructed, you will discover that it's a lot harder to stay on course. Always be aware of the signs along your journey. Not every decision will have a clear choice to make. That's why I believe that prayer and meditation are essential in order to have a discerning spirit. That spiritual guidance will help you figure out what works for you. Then, you and your spouse can work to build and maintain healthy habits that will keep you on the right route and give you the strength you need to continue the climb toward happiness.

7. THE KILLER CREVASSE

The dark, cold mouth of a crevasse is a monster that every ice climber respects and even fears. Sometimes, there are no warning signs before coming face to face with this beast. The crevasse will pull you down in seconds. In the worst-case scenario, you are helpless and alone, crying for help as the gaping abyss swallows you whole, leaving nothing behind except perhaps a memory of your efforts. Climbers know that only a complete focus on self and situational awareness will save them from this nightmare scenario.

What, exactly, is a crevasse? As opposed to a crevice, which is a small hole or a crack that you encounter when rock climbing, a crevasse is more pronounced. It can be found in an ice sheet or on a glacier, and it is a deep crack or fracture created when massive semi-rigid pieces of rock or ice experience different rates of movement. Simply put, it's a massive stress break along the surface causing a gigantic hole in the mountain or glacier of ice. The typical crevasse can easily be over 60ft wide and 150ft in depth, and can stretch across a glacier in any direction. Dangerous in and of itself, but more treacherous because the opening of crevasse can be hidden under a thin layer of snow or ice, causing it to be completely invisible to the climber. This snow bridge blends into the landscape. The sheer weight of a climber can be enough to cause that thin surface to give way and collapse into the crevasse. Even if you survive the fall, you risk suffocation by snow or drowning in the icy water. That is why seasoned mountaineers secure themselves to each other with that dynamic rope mentioned before, in the hope that they will prevent a potentially fatal fall.

As with training to climb an ice mountain, everything you learn about climbing the mountain of marriage needs to be put into action should you ever stumble upon a martial crevasse. There is fierce spiritual warfare against marriages and you must be aware of the forces that are pushing against you. If you are inadequately prepared for a marital crevasse, the fall can take you to the same deep, dark, cold place from which it is nearly impossible to recover.

I have personally encountered and even fallen into a potential *marital killer* crevasse on my journey. Without a focused mindset and proper knowledge about the forces pushing back against marriages, it will be difficult to escape from this chasm. There are those mountaineers who have survived falls such as this, but they were hearty climbers, trained and prepared, who worked well with their partner. Even then, some needed the help of professional rescue climbers. That, too, is a marital lesson and will be covered in the text later. For now, I want to help you learn to interpret and detect the signs of a possible hidden crevasse.

At some point during the first few years Tia and I were married, I drifted from the love I once held for her. I can't tell you the exact moment it began. I was on dangerous ground and about to slip and fall into the belly of a crevasse. Many stressors can break open a marital crevasse, from influence to addictions, but all of them possess a tremendous power of bondage and confusion, unique to each individual. By the time I realized I was trapped deep down in the crevasse, it was too late to simply climb back out. I had lost something critical - my affection for Tia - due to a series of bad decisions I had made.

What does a marital crevasse look like? It can start under the weight of addiction, be it porn, drugs, or even emotional or sexual cheating. That thin cover over the crevasse can be broken with negative thinking about yourself, your situation, your relationship, or your spouse. Day by day, you will slip into these problems without even fully realizing it. Unlike an actual crevasse, this ravine won't be entirely imperceptible; there will be alarms going off in your head. You will sense that something is wrong, but if you are not fully mindful of that first alert, you will ignore subsequent warning signs. It's only when you are totally engulfed in the hole that you will look around and ask, "How did I let this happen?"

When Tia and I tell people about our marriage podcast and its primary focus on helping couples facing a divorce, we receive some surprising responses. "I appreciate it, we are good right now. But if we start having problems, then we will check it out." "We are not even married yet, so we will pass, but thank you." "Our marriage is too messed up, so there's no point." One of the first mistakes that cause people to slip into a marital crevasse is that they don't know they're standing on one. You need to learn how to detect and heed the warning signs. I can tell you firsthand that this type of vital information must be employed, especially if you plan on being married for life.

Scripture reading: Proverbs 28:9
He that turneth away his ear from hearing the law, even his prayer

> *shall be abomination.*

The mission of our podcasts is to not only prevent couples from getting divorced but to also equip couples with some fundamental principles on how to conduct their marriages. We want every couple to become keenly aware of the problems that lead you to divorce, or close to it. By the time a couple is deep into a crevasse, it is not only hard to get out, but some couples never regain enough passion for each other to even try to climb out.

Car manufacturers don't ask you if you want airbags in your car; they equip all vehicles with airbags in case an accident occurs. We have to take the initiative and go a step further with our marriages. If you were facing life or death, such as falling into a crevasse, you would do whatever it takes to prepare yourself for the worst-case scenario. You should treat your marriage with the same passion with which you protect your own life.

Because I have personally experienced and survived this marital crevasse, I was able to discover four stages that I want to share with you regarding "The Killer Crevasse." These stages are: The Probe, The Slip, The Fall and Buried Alive. If you are willing to fight for your marriage, you can recover no matter how deep you are in your marital crevasse. It is possible to come back out on top! But, make no mistake, it won't be easy. The deeper you are, the harder it is to climb out. Hopefully, by understanding that principle and learning to avoid these stages, you will have what it takes to maintain a healthy and happy marriage.

The Probe
During ice climbing, the air temperature will rise and the snow itself will weaken from the heat. Experienced ice climbers know to probe the ground ahead to see if it's safe. They examine the mountain by forcing their ice axe down into the snow to detect if the surface has become too weak to walk on. If the axe goes too far or

the surface seems too loose, the climber knows there is a possible hidden crevasse. The climber must be well-trained to decipher both when probing is necessary and when the feel of the axe head landing in the snow is off.

Every day, we all are continually probing the situations in our lives for clues. The primitive reptilian parts of our brain kick in and analyze if a situation is safe or a threat. Probing is a natural way of life. Whether we engage in a casual conversation or have a big decision to make, our choices and actions can either help or hurt our marriage. Having discernment is a gift from God. He wants us to spiritually consider every situation in our life to make sure we are always making the best choices.

Scripture reading: John 14:16-17

16 *And I will ask the Father, and he will give you another advocate to help you and be with you forever—*

17 *the Spirit of Truth. The world cannot accept him, because it neither sees him nor knows him. But you know him, for he lives with you and will be in you*

The Spirit is the initial warning sign to which I referred earlier. When we probe our day-to-day lives and find that a situation isn't good for us, we can either listen to that spiritual discernment or ignore it. This is the gift of free will. But the more we fail, the more we ignore the right decision, the more numb we become to the voice of the Spirit. In John 14:16-17, Jesus is speaking to his disciples and He talks about the Spirit of Truth residing inside of us. As long as we are consistently listening for and obeying that still small voice, we will have the Truth remain firmly inside of us, prompting us to make the right decisions.

The problem in life and marriage is that many of us fall short in the choices we make. When a person continually makes the wrong choices, the Spirit of Truth will become very quiet to them. "For the wages of sin is death; but the gift of God is eternal life through Jesus Christ our Lord." -Romans 6:23. Most people mistake this death as a physical death; in fact, it refers to a spiritual death. As you become numb to true wisdom, you start down a very dark path, diametrically opposed to the path from which you started, and it is this passageway that will cause you to slip.

The Slip

A few years ago, I went for a drink with a friend. It started as a normal night out. Great music, social environment and to top it off, the "Dirty Birds" were whooping the "Cowgirls". But after more than a couple of glasses of beer, and getting a loose mouth, I mentioned to my friend that I thought our waitress was cute. Impulsively, my friend went over to the waitress and told her what I had said. When he returned, I told him that I wished he hadn't done that. But because we were both drinking, we simply laughed it off and went about our business. However, only 15 minutes later, the young lady came to our table and told me that although she didn't have time to talk while she was working, she would love for me to give her a call sometime. And she gave me her number.

Though I was still shocked that the young lady had done this, I brashly told my friend I was going to call her. He was taken aback, said he was only trying to embarrass me and never thought she would give me her number. A simple statement – "our waitress is cute" - started a chain of decisions and actions which would cause me to slip.

Up to that point in my marriage, I had never put myself in this type of position. I knew that if I did something foolish like that, I would have a hard time stopping myself. Because I made a comment at the wrong time, around the wrong person, I had put myself and my marriage on a path toward destruction. But that wasn't clear to me back then. I had convinced myself that it was all harmless when clearly it wasn't. I told myself I would just have a little fun. My friend kept telling me to get rid of the number. Yet, wrong things have a tendency to feel good at the time, to feel right. This risky behavior made me feel as if I were single and free again.

An idea gains power and manifests into reality when you say something or take some sort of action. We are continually having thoughts, some good, some bad. When you develop a harmful thought, you have a clear choice. You can act on that thought or let it pass. If that thought doesn't serve you, if you want to stay safe, let it pass. It's not easy, but it is totally doable. With proper mindful techniques, you can learn to strengthen that mental muscle.

It's important to remember that a negative thought can have real-world consequences if acted upon. So, if we acknowledge that a thought is bad for us, then we should think it through and understand the negative consequences. Instead, many of us give in to temptation, conjure up all the reasons it will feel good, and try to justify that feeling good is okay. In essence, we need to learn how to take control of our thoughts.

A study from the University of Groningen demonstrated that when you listen to happy music, you tend to see more happy, smiling faces throughout your day. But when you listen to sad music, the opposite is true. This study proved that with the power of your mind, you can control how you interpret your environment. Utilize this power to help prevent a slip. Become intentional with your thoughts and what you do with them, whether it involves a disloyal act toward your spouse or yourself.

At the time of the waitress incident, I was unaware of how to control my thoughts. I allowed myself to think of all the ways that doing something wrong would make me feel good, temporarily. I let my thoughts run away and those thoughts controlled my actions. Eventually, I gave in to the idea of following my fleshly desires. Anyone can slip. It may be big like mine or on a smaller scale. At this stage of our journey, we can recover quicker by taking control of our thoughts and recognizing how negative thoughts can lead us on a path toward negative results.

The Fall

After I received that phone number from the waitress, I decided I would text her the next day, against my friend's continuous warnings. I knew it wasn't the smartest idea but I had continued to rationalize the concept. She agreed to meet me and we hung out a few times. Fortunately, I didn't let it go further than kissing. But, clearly, I fell for the trap I had set for myself. In my head, I believed with sincerity that I could handle a casual conversation with this attractive woman who was not my wife. Even writing this here causes me a facepalm moment. I thought I could tempt fate without crossing any boundaries, not realizing that the moment I gave in to that negative thought, the line had already been crossed.

Donnell had started to leave the home more and more. I was so jealous of his ability to go out and have a life outside of he and I. I thought this new life was replacing the life we built together. I felt alone as I was learning how to navigate my new body. The first child was one thing, but this time I felt entirely like a new woman. Nothing to be ashamed of, but I simply felt like I was in a foreign body. While at home, I was dealing with a toddler and a newborn and my husband was out with friends trying to figure out how we ended up here. I started to get these heavy feelings of anxiousness in my chest. They say a woman's intuition is a force not to reckon with. I continued the days hoping the feeling would go away but it simply wouldn't. I thought about my

sisters, my mother, my father, my friends, and then it dawned on me that it might be my husband. After all, he had been acting strange the last few days, being mysteriously absent from the home many hours before and after work. I thought I suspected that he was stressed but never did I expect what soon came after.

Change was coming for me and I was not ready for it at all. One day, while I was fast asleep, my phone went off. I had received a text from this young lady I had been secretly seeing. Not just a text; it was a full-blown video of her saying that she misses me and can't wait to see me again. It was straight out of a movie. Because I was asleep when the text came in, I wasn't the one who heard it first. I woke up this loud crash and saw my wife, Tia, standing at our bedroom door. "What happened?" I asked, not knowing about the text. Tia stood there, silently. Continued to stare at me. "What's wrong?" I asked. I didn't know what was going on, but I knew it wasn't good.

"Don't act like you don't know!" she responded.

At that point, the pieces fell into place and I realized she might have found out about this other woman. But even then I didn't come clean. I tried to be this *player*, a character my wrong thinking had convinced me to become, so I played stupid. We continued to stare at each other for an uncomfortable time, with me looking confused and she looking hurt and angry. I casually looked for my phone. That's when I noticed it was out of its case, and the screen was cracked. I knew I had been caught.

I was so hurt at Donnell's actions I couldn't even scream at him. It was like I was staring in the mirror screaming but nothing was coming out. The loud crash even surprised me and I realized his phone flying from my grasp and into the wall. The high rise condo we lived in had cement walls. The case shattered into

pieces and from there I froze. Once I found out this news, the lump that was once in my chest suddenly went into my throat as I burst into tears.

That feeling of dread, not knowing what comes next, was one of the worst feelings in the world. And then Tia said it out loud and confirmed my suspicion.

"Who is she?" my wife asked, growing angrier and offended.

"Who is who?" I responded, trying to fake some level of ignorance. I knew it was a stupid question as soon as I said it, but I had panicked.

"The girl who texted your phone saying she misses you?" she said. I knew what was done in the dark was now coming to light.

You could have heard a pin drop. I had no real defense, no plausible explanation or excuse. I knew I had made the first big mistake within our marriage, and at that moment, I feared it could likely be the last mistake I would make. Here's the worst part: I knew all the while that it was utterly wrong as I was doing it. I knew it when I had lied to my wife several times about where I was going. I simply could have stopped just by having that negative gut feeling. Honestly, at that point, it was best she found me out. Even though I had convinced myself that I was going to cut things off with this waitress, that was only a plan. I could have easily picked up where we had left off. And God only knows how far I would have let it go.

It's worth pointing out that this lady didn't care a hoot about my marriage. In fact, that was never on her, it was my job 100%. It's unfair to blame the other person when I had lost sight of my path and my purpose. As a result, I was headed straight toward a fall.

The fall felt like it would last forever. While finding out about the emotional affair, I could not fully blame the "other woman" for stepping into my husband's space. The commitment was made between him and I and he had violated the covenant he made with me and with God. I left our home and went to stay with family so that I could decide if I wanted to stay married. I thought about what made my husband have an emotional affair in the first place. Where did we go wrong? The reality is that there were so many forces stacked against us that I couldn't imagine the feeling of being trapped he must have felt. I had to be honest with myself. I never gave him the satisfaction to think that his mistake was justified, but I prayed for God to reveal my own mistakes in this situation as well. I realized that I was a different person than when we first met. Initially, I was sweet and kind, and nurturing. I allowed him into my space and treated him like a man. I uplifted his character and gave him the hope that he could lead us to victory. But after experiencing grief, financial burdens, and postpartum depression, I was a shell. Living to live, and not to experience all that life has to offer. I was cold, distant, and disengaged. I would hold the kids only for the comfort of my grief, I would demand attention from Donnell that he felt he could never give enough of. Slowly, I pushed him away. If we had the tools to know how to fight through the trials life would take us through we could have avoided many problems. I understand that any infidelity
is a hard pill to swallow, but I wanted to be sure that I did the best I could do before allowing my husband to take all of the blame.

It took some time for Tia and I to move past my mistake. And still today, I'm sure it upsets my wife when she is reminded of it. But in coming back from that, in climbing out of that pit, I've learned that I need to try every day to let her know how much I love her. I also need to work at the relationship, to give my wife a sense of security and loyalty. I have become painfully aware of the decisions I make, and how the smallest of seemingly innocent choices can create some of the biggest problems. It's not an easy task to recover from this stage. As you learn to discipline yourself in controlling your own thoughts, though, it gets easier and easier until your mindset is naturally changed.

Did this slip mean that I didn't love my wife anymore? No. I still loved her. But I got caught up in my own head, and because of my wrong focus, I fell hard! I had stopped spending time with my wife and invested my time in other places. At first, I thought it was all harmless. But when we neglect our spouse and invest our time elsewhere, the ROI (return on investment) from that neglect will come in the form of destruction and reduction.

Have you ever noticed all the places from which weeds grow? We're so accustomed to seeing them in the most random places that we don't really notice them unless they are in our own backyard. Weeds have the power to grow out of the cracks in roads, sidewalks, driveways, just about anywhere. They do not need planting or nurturing. Weeds grow everywhere, and once established, it's tough to get rid of them. In our minds, weeds are like those errant or corrupt thoughts. They can crop up anytime, anywhere. We have to be prepared to deal with them right away or they can overrun our thoughts.

If we are not consciously aware of the thoughts and decisions we make, we will allow these harmful situations in our lives to become fully manifest. And by the time we notice that we have made an awful decision, it's going to be that much harder to clean up our mistakes. Some people never even get a chance to rewrite their mistakes. Just like evil thoughts are the unwanted ideas in our heads, weeds are the most unwelcome type of plants. Our minds have the power to grow and flourish like a beautiful garden. Yet, if we leave the mind or our garden unattended or fail to take well-ordered steps, we can end up surrounded by a whole lot of mistakes that have grown out of bad habits.

Buried Alive

One of the fears an ice climber faces is that after slipping and falling into a crevasse, they could be buried by an avalanche of snow and ice. The amount of snow can vary, but anything that puts you in further danger once you've fallen inside reduces your chances of getting out alive. There have been instances when a climber has escaped out of a crevasse even after being buried by an avalanche. But this hazardous and life-threatening situation is to be avoided at all costs.

I'd like to say that I haven't been down this far, that I'm only speaking hypothetically, but that would be a lie. In fact, there was a desperately low point in my married life where I found myself at rock bottom, covered over with mistakes. Tia and I had decided that for us, divorce was our best path forward. I was mentally exhausted and felt that I had no one to talk to about my situation. I tried to get my head around where I was, but I could not for the life of me figure out how I fell so far from where I had started off in my marriage. Not only did I feel utterly defeated, I no longer thought I should be married at all. In my own state of self-loathing, I convinced myself that Tia could have done so much better than me and that I was just wasting her time.

You see, I lowered my standards the day I decided to talk to another woman. And I continued to lower my guard and increase my own vulnerability over and over again. I had also developed a bad habit of thinking that this lifestyle was okay. I was buried, covered in my sins and mistakes. Acts of infidelity, addictions, argumentativeness, aggressiveness, and even isolation all drew me away from Tia, physically, emotionally, and spiritually. I had somehow convinced myself that I wasn't in love anymore. And I simply wanted us both to move on.

Even during our separation, I started talking to other women. I looked for ways to make the transition easier for myself, picking up more unhealthy habits and creating a further destructive mindset. I even blamed my current situation on my last marriage. Perhaps I was carrying too much mental baggage, maybe I would never even be able to love anyone again.

Our minds determine exactly how we perceive the world around us. We can choose to witness God's beautiful and vast creation, or we can dig ourselves deep within a mental crevasse of our own creation, buried with feelings of suffocation. This sensation is similar to the feeling of having a severe case of anxiety or a panic attack. But it doesn't matter how big the world or how burdensome our problem. If we tell ourselves that there is no space left to breathe, then that's how our world or environment will look and feel.

I mentioned before that I couldn't tell you the exact moment that I found myself slipping down. But it was evident. Anytime we make even the smallest decisions that do not serve us or our purpose, we will watch life as we know it reshape itself around us. The mind stores everything deep inside so we don't really forget, we push it down deeper into our subconscious. And we tend to work hard to forget those unhealthy steps that led us to the point of no return. By the time we ask ourselves what went wrong, we've completely restructured our mental hardware, and our beliefs end up changing.

Today, I see so many couples at this point in their marriage. They have grown apart from their spouse and have likely even picked up destructive or abusive habits. They make excuses for their poor decisions, work hard at justifying their reasons for choosing to divorce. If you ask them if they still want to be married, most will likely say no. Whenever physical abuse plays a role in a marriage, there is a need for physical separation, but ultimately, divorce was never God's desire for us. And it shouldn't be a desire for ourselves.

No sane person stands up in front of God and everyone and declares a lifelong commitment with their partner, with the intention to divorce them sometime later. You don't have to be married to recognize that the breakup of a marriage, through divorce, will cut deep. It can create permanent emotional damage. But if divorce should not be a considered option, is it possible to get back to the level of love we once had for our partner? Yes, you can! If a person decides to turn their situation around, they can climb out of the crevasse. Just like I did. Now, there are different shapes and sizes when it comes to a marital crevasse, and each unique situation will need to be dealt with on a case by case basis. I've been deep at the bottom of the marital crevasse. And together with my wife, my buddy, we lifted our marriage out of that cold, dark place. With the right coaching, a sincere desire to climb out of the pit, and a genuine willingness to submit to the process, you, too, can experience emotional restoration and healing. You can truly save your marriage.

8. THE FIGHTING PURPOSE

A recent study done by the National Health Service found that grandparents who babysit their grandchildren live longer than ones who don't. If you understand the psychology behind having a purpose, this makes perfect sense. "Purpose" is essential to our very nature. It's a driving force that keeps us going forward when we are too tired to continue. It allows us to continue fighting, even when we are weak. When you work to set goals and establish values, you create your purpose and in doing so, you surround yourself with positive emotions.

Before I understood what God's divine purpose was for my marriage, Tia and I simply went through the motions. We knew what we wanted to do, more or less, but we didn't know precisely how to go about it. It seemed as if *everything* we tried failed. Eventually, I realized that we had never asked God what our divine purpose was. After Tia and I decided to get a divorce, I asked her if she would join me in a spiritual fast before we made this big decision. Even though the divorce was my decision, I still wanted to do everything I could before calling it quits for good.

During our fast, I met with Marvin, the pastor of The Ark church in Gwinnett County, Georgia and a genuine godly friend, as well as a mentor of mine. He asked me a simple but profound question, one which changed the course of my family's future. He asked me if I knew what God's will was for my marriage. But I wasn't ready to hear anything like that. Even fasting about the decision turned out to be harder than expected. I already knew that getting a divorce was against God's will and that it was my own will that was driving my desire to end the marriage. That was never in God's plan for me. Though I was somewhat resistant to the notion of exploring what God wanted for me, I relented. As head of my household, I felt deep down inside that I needed to make every effort, to explore all available options before abandoning my marriage and breaking up my family.

When I finally confessed and told Marvin that I didn't know what God's will was for my marriage, he challenged me with this response: ask God for the answer. Sounds simple enough. Of course, God doesn't communicate in the ways that we do. No texting. No email. As if we would listen to Him anyway. I discovered that when it comes to asking God for something, it's more important to connect with Him.

Connecting with anyone can be difficult, especially if you've never spoken with them or even met them before. When you meet a total stranger and attempt to build a relationship with them, you have set rules for that encounter. You won't share anything too intimate, such as the bedwetting incident at a sleepover, the crush on your third-grade math teacher, or the addiction you keep secret. You might share some light-hearted stories that don't really give away the *real* you. You keep a barrier between the two of you, only giving out so much information, and you accept their stories from a casual distance, feigning interest in how their cat is doing after the hairball removal surgery. If you get too close to them, they may get too close to you. We keep our connections at arms length, in an outer circle, until we believe we can establish trust. Sometimes, we know them solely on a surface level, and vice versa, and we are okay with that.

Every once in a while, we let someone get a little bit closer. We can still get hurt when we do that, so we stay guarded. We almost never share everything with them. Maybe, we'll lie to them so they don't get offended or upset; we may even reveal a little too much about our private self and risk them running away. That's the human condition. We can't read each other's thoughts, so we are only as truthful and connected as our personal safety threshold allows. We are rarely as connected to one another on a more intimate basis. Even on social media, we create an alternate reality of ourselves that protects us from letting others know what we really think or feel. We give them what they want to hear and offer only the parts of ourselves that we feel is safe for them to know. Nothing more.

Our relationship with God, though, is entirely different. It doesn't matter what you tell Him; He already knows the truth. He knows every thought you've ever had, every word you've ever spoken, and every single thing you've ever done. The Bible says that He knew us when we were still in our mothers' wombs. God has had an omniscient eye on you since before you were born. So, when you tell Him you had a bad day, He already knows; you tell Him so that you can get it off your chest. He wants to hug you and tell you it will be alright, to help you deal with it. No matter what circumstance, you don't have to worry about the bad things you think, say, or do because God knows everything about you and still loves you.

That needs repeating. God loves you. Always. Without question. When you accept His Son, Jesus, as your personal Lord and Savior, there is NOTHING that you can do to make Him stop loving you.

In fact, He still loves you when you haven't asked Jesus into your heart. He loves you that much. He knows what really happened to your little brother's toy car, and He still loves you. Even if your brother hasn't forgiven you some twenty years later.

The truth is that connecting with God is so much easier than connecting with anyone else on Earth. He's already got the 4-1-1 on you, and now you've got the lowdown on Him, too. His very nature is to connect with us because he made us in his image. He loves us more than we can love Him back, and His love is infinite. Start from there, and it will be a whole lot easier to open up. Besides, He already knows your wants and needs. Asking is your way of opening up to hear His answer.

For me to connect with God and seek His guidance meant that I would need to spend a lot more time connecting with Him. My best approach is through fasting, prayer, and purposefully searching through the Bible. This was how I approached my quest to understand what His Word says about divorce. During the time I seeked His purpose, I discovered what He wanted from me and I found the real purpose of my marriage, too. Then, I shifted to pray for strength and wisdom. If I was going to be able to fulfill His will, I needed His divine direction. And thus, the sincere search of my own heart began.

I began to understand that because of my actions and choices, I had become part of my generation's growing statistic of failed marriages. I hated the idea of living my life that way. This would have been my second divorce. If I didn't try and fight for this one, then I would be subconsciously repeating the same patterns. With this realization, my purpose became more prominent than my problems. And instead of me wondering if my marriage would work, I started working on my marriage.

I am convinced that in discovering my purpose - God's purpose for me - I saved my marriage. This journey, and grace from God, has given me the passion to fulfill that purpose and help other married couples save their relationships. Now, Tia and I work together to advocate for other troubled marriages. We openly share our struggles and triumphs to inspire couples and we offer them coaching so that they can build a stronger bond. Tia and I sought God's counsel, we developed an understanding of our purpose, and we discovered His gifts planted within ourselves.

Living your purpose is very important. So many couples get together with no drive, no shared or common direction. This lack of purpose will cause them to hit a dead end at some point in their relationship. If an idle mind is the devil's workshop, then you must occupy your mind with something bigger than yourself to ensure that your mind is purposefully busy. When you have a sense of purpose, like that grandchild to a grandparent, you have a relentless drive toward a shared goal. This sets the foundation for you to become a power couple.

How can you find your purpose if you don't already have one? Well, as tried and tested Marriage Mountaineers, Tia and I offer coaching to help our students find their purpose. Here, we share some ideas to help get you started. So, ready yourselves, fasten your climbing harnesses, sharpen your focus and let's embark on a journey to take your relationship to new heights.

First, as a unit, a couple bound in Holy Matrimony, allow yourselves to mentally detach from your external environment. Don't develop a personal or family goal based on what people say you should do or possess. Your purpose needs to be something that complements who you are and the gifts you have. So, silence that outer noise, eliminate all of the worldly distractions, and listen intently to the desires that God has placed upon your heart. Don't strive for what you think you want, or feel some sort of conscious desire to attain, but open up yourself to become a vessel. Be willing to accept the work of a greater force that works within and through you for a purpose greater than self.

Carefully monitor your influences. As unpleasant as it sounds, you must limit your social media time. You may need to cut off social media entirely, at least until you find your purpose. I have spent years trying to find what works for me. Each time I thought I had it under control, I would get caught up in another new social media venture. If I had a nickel for every time I was convinced to start an MLM company, I would be a wealthy man.The people who are very gifted at convincing you to join their journey or business model know how to hit you where you're most vulnerable: "the lack of money." Remember that money is simply a form of energy and it will come, almost effortlessly, once you find your purpose. As a couple, you will get so caught up in doing what you love that any money you receive will be an added bonus.

Scripture reading: Matthew 7:7

Ask and it will be given to you; seek and you will find; knock and the door will be opened to you

---

Once you have eliminated the external distractions, pat your-selves on the back. Congratulations! You have taken the first step toward becoming conscious, or as some would say, "woke." This is the time when you need to start seeking divine direction. Prayer, meditation, and patience are the tools that will enable you to find your purpose. When you allow yourself to become too attached to an idea, you don't leave room to hear from God. He wants to share with you His deepest secrets and plans. But you have to ask Him to share them with you first. As the scriptures say, If you ask, He will answer! Even if what you are currently doing fulfills the divine purpose for your life, it doesn't hurt to seek further con-firmation. Open your heart and learn to listen to that still, small voice, every single day. Life is constantly changing, and you want to make sure you are adapting to your environment in the phys-ical and spiritual realms.

It's essential to understand the difference between the concepts of passion and purpose. Passion is doing what you love. Whereas, "purpose" is doing something that contributes to a greater good. For example, I spent several years of my life focused primarily on pursuing music and film. I absolutely love expressing myself through art. I knew that one day, I would do that full time because it was more than just my hobby. But, I also needed to make money doing it. The problem was, I never had a purpose to my pursuit of art. I went after that dream because it made me feel good and whole, but I was not really thinking about who it could help. When I attached the idea of helping and coaching people with their marriages, I finally figured out how I could connect my heart's passion to my higher purpose. I decided to use my artistic gifts to inspire people by creating positive, motivating content. Now, not only can I enjoy doing something that I genuinely love, but since there is a legitimate purpose behind it, I have a clear vision on how to implement my passion.

My goal for the Mountaineer Marriage book and the follow-on activities is to use positivity to promote healthy relationships through personalized training and education. It's ironic that the entire time I was working on musical pieces or visual illustrations, I thought those God-given gifts existed to provide for me. In fact, those gifts are intended to help serve my purpose. When I finally began to work harder at bringing them both together, I learned that I could share my positive message better. Now, I can do it in a way that reaches out to a much broader audience. This was all made possible because of my skills and talents. I had been blessed with these gifts and had nurtured them for many years. When I finally focused on my true purpose, when I shared my message by using my gifts, I received a greater bonus than I could have imagined.

At the point when you genuinely believe you have discovered

your purpose, discuss it with your spouse. This is important for several reasons. First, see if your spouse can offer some level of confirmation for you. Explain as best you can about your new path forward. If it is truly destined from God, then He will reveal it to your spouse, assuming that they are listening to Him. If the two of you are not aligned in this vision, it will most likely fail. Therefore, make sure that you both are in full agreement about what you need to do as a family. Your spouse may have talents and gifts that will complement your own and make the perfect team as you move along the trail toward your purpose. It may take a little work for you both to come together. However, once your partner understands your shared vision and purpose, you can figure out how to join together to achieve great things. Your work together will grow each of your gifts as you also grow your relationship. Of course, not every couple can blend together like Beyonce and Jay-Z, dominating an industry. But, without a doubt, you can share the journey with your spouse, climbing the mountain together by complementing one another's gifts.

It's critical to include your spouse in your fundamental purpose. When I thought my wife's purpose was *just* serving in the US military, I had shared an idea with her to produce video content for the spouses of deployed military members. It would serve as a way for the service members to express their love during their absence, like a video postcard. Yet, that ultimately was not on our route up the mountain. We learned, as you will, that you need to have a vision for your marriage which is more significant than yourselves. Possibly, you may find that you have the same shared purpose, as my wife and I do. Or, you may each have different or separate purposes. Yet, as I explained in Chapter 4, your journey should still come together, and you should complement each other in your life's mission. This will give your marriage a tremendous boost. Its own life, as it were. We are all spiritual beings, called to join together as one, in marriage. The flesh will fail you. Absolutely. You'll make mistakes, have missteps, and yes, even doubts. But, if you open your heart to being part of a grand divine purpose, then you will experience a marriage like no other. Climbing Marriage Mountain together will be a journey that will last a lifetime, and as you move up the path, you will become a bright light on that hill, inspiring others to do the same!

9. ICE-SAR RESCUE

Icelandic Association for Search and Rescue (Ice-SAR) is a national association of rescue units located in, you guessed it, Iceland. They specialize in both accident prevention as well as search and rescue. The organization has team members present in most towns across the nation of Iceland and consists of roughly 10,000 volunteers. These individuals are volunteers, and as such, are not paid by the government. Since some of the volunteers operate in a full-time capacity and require a lot of equipment, training, and supplies, they are supported through charitable donations and various fundraising activities. The units are thoroughly trained and educated in their fields to handle both dangerous land and sea rescue missions. The organization and their efforts are widely respected, as their members and groups are held to very high standards. Because they coordinate rescue groups dealing with land, sea, diving, high-angle rescue, and even search dogs, they are expertly equipped to handle any type of emergency rescue situation.

When my marriage was faltering, my mentor reached out his hand to help. He dedicated his time to assist me in determining not only what I perceived as the problem, but the real risks to ending my marriage. He made clear what I was giving up by walking away from Tia. I had convinced myself that I needed to throw in the towel. I saw a marriage that had reached its peak and was on its inevitable slide. A big part of the problem? I didn't understand what a marriage really is. And I didn't know exactly what I was leaving behind.

In giving up on my family, I would have given up my destiny. My future. Sure, it's fair to say that when one door closes, another opens. But, how much time do we waste by allowing so many doors to close simply because we choose to give up on a divine destiny? In the midst of a storm and all its chaos, it's easy to miss the call of destiny on your life. Our more primitive emotions tend to control our thinking and cloud our thoughts to such an extent that when we gaze up at the mountain, we are blinded to our higher purpose.

Because my mentor spent so much time reframing my mind, I was able to change the direction from the path of divores by becoming aware of the fact that divorce was not truly a promising option. He coached me on the steps I needed to take to save my marriage. Because I wanted to try everything before I got a divorce, I was open to hearing what my mentor had to say. I felt that it was my responsibility to take action to heal us. As long as Tia was willing to save the marriage, I needed to try, especially since, for most of the marriage, I was the one in the wrong.

I fell deep into a crevasse by not being intentional with my thoughts and actions. It wasn't easy to climb back out, but at the very last moment, I received a lifeline from someone who cared enough about healed marriages. If you have a desire to fight and a humbled heart, help will come for you. Make sure you are willing to accept that helping hand.

Today, Tia and I dedicate all our efforts to coach other marriages. I consider the two of us to be a lot like ICE-SAR. No doubt, we are still learning a lot about marriage and each other, and there are many who are higher up the mountain than we are. My mentor stepped in for Tia and me when we were further down the mountain, struggling to make it up, and guided us so we could continue our climb and make it to the summit. Now, when we see other couples struggling, we can do the same.

Getting rescued can be a humbling experience. Everyone has to sacrifice something for it to work. Sometimes, when climbers go up the mountain, they become lost and disoriented, and it's difficult for them to admit they are lost. That's the first sacrifice we all must accept when we are struggling in any area of our lives. If you don't admit that you need assistance, confess it, as it were, help won't be able to come. You have to call out on the phone, or radio, or shoot up that flare, so people will know that you need and want help. If they don't see your struggle, if you don't set down your pride and call out, the rescue can't begin.

Once you admit you need help, someone needs to be willing to step up. Many around you have good intentions, but they are not equipped for the job. Not everyone is a rescue swimmer. As a former lifeguard, I can attest that you have to be specially trained in how to deal with people who are drowning. Even though they ask for help, they can be a danger in the water to anyone around them. They can unintentionally knock a lifeguard unconscious or, in a panic, pull you under with them. This is why you want someone who understands how to help you. Tia and I are trained relationship coaches at Mountaineer Marriage. We have the proper training and preparation to help when someone reaches out their hand.

When you are in crisis, it's important to follow the rescuer's instructions. If something goes wrong on a climb, the worst thing you can do is refuse to listen to the rescuer. If they tell you to step here, cut that line, or let go of that grip, trust that they are giving you the best possible advice to save you. If there is time and the threat is not immediate, you can ask questions. But if your danger is urgent, listen and respond immediately. If an avalanche is coming you need to get to a safer place, you can't hesitate and wait until you're comfortable. While it's not the military, this is a time to jump when they say jump and ask how high on your way up. (I still don't know how they do that, but that's apparently how they are taught)

Once you are rescued, give thanks. Rescuers aren't looking for your gratitude, but they will appreciate a sincere thank you. Walk around with a heart of thanksgiving, of appreciation. Pay it forward. If you see someone struggling, don't sit by and watch them fall into a crevasse. You can't save the world, but you can ask if they need help, and if you are not in a position to assist, find someone who can. Every time you help someone, you create an opportunity for them to pay it forward. One after another, we can grow a helping community and watch healing take place. Let us all become Marriage Mountain Rescue Advocates.

There's an old saying that a penny saved is a penny earned. It means that if you can find a cheaper way to do something, it gives you more money to spend. A pretty smart way to manage money. So, what is the value of a saved marriage? I can attest that had my marriage not been saved, its demise would have especially affected my children's lives. There's only such much failure, rejection, and heartbreak any of us can withstand. In the words of Sade, "How many loves inside, I can't say." None of us know how much pain we can tolerate. How can we begin to guess for others? I know that if Tia and I saved a marriage like ours, we can create opportunities for great things to happen in marriages, no matter the circumstance. Tia and I use the hurt, pain, and experience of our rescue to bring others out of their crevasse. That's far more valuable than a penny or two. When I look at how happy and joyful my wife and daughters are now, I am filled with an immeasurable sense of pride and accomplishment. It may be better to have loved and lost than never loved, but it's far better to love - and win!

Few people work as hard as the rescuers at ICE-SAR to train for a situation they hope to never use. The sacrifice they make reminds me of an incident that occurred when I was in high school. One of our deans disappeared one day. There was no notice, no announcement. The police didn't start interrogating students. One day, a few students noticed that he wasn't around. They mentioned it to their friends, and around the school it went. Soon, most of us noticed his absence and yet, no one knew where he was. It was as if he had simply vanished. Eventually, the mystery was solved when we learned that our dean was a reservist in the military. He had been called up for deployment. Prior to this, we students considered him just another ordinary school administrator. No one knew this other side of him. But to the military, he was a soldier. And they had made him ready to be called at a moment's notice in service to our country.

Being an advocate for marriages may not seem as noble as being part of the military or being an ICE-SAR rescuer. But to breaking or broken hearts inside of a failing marriage, a loving word of encouragement can be a life saver. When I was working my 'regular' day job, I would occasionally have to stop and offer advice to someone in need. Sometimes, it was a co-worker asking for help with their own troubled marriage or that of their parents; sometimes, it was a customer who was at their wit's end and felt compelled to spill out their heart and tell their whole life's story. I made myself available while still respecting the responsibilities of my workplace because my divine purpose is to talk about the love of God and the power of healing! Being a good marriage coach starts with having an empathetic spirit. You must feel compelled to aid individuals and couples in need. If the marriage community is going to turn the tide of failed marriages, then we must become like the ICE-SAR volunteers. We all need to allow ourselves to be open and ready at any moment to help another couple in need while also doing what we can to keep our own marriages healthy. I believe we can create the community that I was searching for years ago, and I am sure that we will find many advocates as well as people who are searching for help.

Marriage is priceless; it's worth more than our jobs, our bank accounts, our possessions. Marriage is not only a holy and sacred institution, it is also a key mechanism by which God perfects us and develops us as individuals and as a team. Perhaps you've heard the saying that, "Behind every great man is a greater woman?" The truth is that a husband and wife who are committed to a noble cause and are rooted in following Biblical principles will succeed.

Success does not necessarily look the same from couple to couple. It could mean keeping their kids connected to God. Or helping fund their children's education. Or it could mean they are destined to launch a worldwide multimedia empire, to spread love and hope to married couples everywhere.

Marriage isn't trivial; it's essential. Marriage isn't a man-made idea; it's a promise from God. Marriage isn't another hobby to put on a shelf; it's a Holy Covenant meant to be respected and cherished at all costs. Marriage isn't a burden; it's a heavenly gift. Marriage isn't about self-sacrifice; it's about a shared commitment and purpose. And marriage isn't a high cost; it's a source of power, success, and wealth. Keep that thought uppermost in your mind: marriage is wealth. Not just monetary but wealthy in mindset. If you fight for your marriage and the marriages of others, you will be blessed, they will be blessed, and partners will succeed in what they come together to achieve.

10. THE SUMMIT

The highest point of a mountain is called a summit. At an elevation of 29,029 ft, Mt. Everest is the highest summit in the world. Mountaineers who climb Mt. Everest stay at the Everest base camp for a few weeks solely to get acclimated to the thin air before they make the climb. Because climbers can suffer from an oxygen-starved delirium, they employ an additional source of support - a professional guide whose expertise is critical for their very survival.

As climbers make their way toward the top of this imposing monster of a mountain, they report feeling morose and morbid when they pass the mile marker. This is the mountain's death zone and it's littered with the corpses of fallen climbers. The scene is a continual reminder that even well-trained climbers, with the best available gear, and led by highly experienced Everest guides, can lose their lives on the journey. In fact, the primary cause of death for Everest climbers are those unavoidable avalanches.

I have witnessed marriages all around me fail. Most of the time, one of the spouses, if not both, proceeds to justify their reasoning for their decision. They confidently state their grounds for this change in course.

"She doesn't respect me."

"I don't love him anymore."

"I made a mistake."

"I'm in love with someone else."

I've heard so many similar excuses over the years that generally fall into a small handful of categories. They have a sense that they have been wronged by their spouse. Or they feel that their spouse is lacking, or not enough for them. Or perhaps they feel as if the marriage thing is just not for them. The focus is rarely on the two of them together, but on each as individuals. It's as if the right hand is saying that it is not compatible with the left hand, and vice versa. What both spouses fail to see is that they are totally compatible and part of a larger purpose.

The underlying message of these excuses tells me that there is a fundamental lack of strength or will to continue to fight for the relationship. Perhaps, in our culture, the idea that there is a permanence to marriage is fading. Here along our journeys, we now witness these broken couples and damaged hearts, casualties of the climb like those lifeless bodies along the trail up Mt. Everest.

This is not meant to scare anyone. It is intended to convey an important reminder, one that needs to stay top of mind. Be aware of the seriousness of the decision when you plan to make your way up a dangerous mountain such as Mt. Everest. Though the panorama from the summit is beautiful beyond words, you can't spend more than a few minutes taking in the view because the air is so thin. All that work to enjoy a few moments of beauty and then start the several-hour descent back down to the base camp!

The lesson here is that the top of the mountain is never meant to be your ultimate destination. It's merely a stop along a life-long journey. Sure, you can take a break and look back and enjoy where you've come from, but you need to continue your journey with your partner and climb to new heights. Along the way, even if you step on some of the same paths you've already traveled, you're a different couple. You've grown closer, stronger, and more skilled to take on new challenges.

One year, I decided to buy a drone for my film production. When I flew it for the first time, I instantly fell in love with the experience. It was remarkable to view the world from above, like getting an entirely new perspective. Imagine if we could get that same perspective on our marriage! What would you see? A stagnant relationship? Or one that is growing and developing? Perhaps you have made it to the top of a mountain. Take time to relish in the accomplishment! Make note of how high and far you've come, but always remember that your journey doesn't stop there.

Though Tia and I have made it to the top of Marriage Mountain, there are more mountains for us to climb. Now, we enjoy the view from wherever we are and look forward to the journey ahead. Your journey up Marriage Mountain will make you a more experienced climber and you will be able to share what you've learned. Take that experience and share it; give advice to others about the best path to hike, what obstacles or trails to watch out for, and any unforeseen avalanches. Your knowledge and wisdom can prevent others from making the same mistake you did. This is a golden opportunity to save others from experiencing undo pain and heartache, and I hope you feel compelled to pay it forward.

Unfortunately, I didn't have the initial support I needed to navigate the trail through my marriage. I suspect that most people feel that men have it all together and know how to lead a family, but this lack isn't apparent until things take a wrong turn. Despite the hazards of the trail on which I had started, I did not allow my journey to become a sad story. I took responsibility for myself and my marriage. I began to educate myself more about the psychological reasons behind the mistakes of my marriage. I prayed for guidance and wisdom. I specifically sought out successful mentors through their books and media. I made a very mature and conscious decision to keep fighting for my marriage. And I did all of these steps while questioning whether or not I wanted to be in a committed relationship anymore.

Is it possible to make your marriage work even after one or both of you don't want it anymore? If you or your partner are at this point, you may be thinking, "This is pointless." Perhaps you feel that our story is irrelevant or not applicable to your personal situation. You may believe that you can't move past where you are, that Tia and I had miraculously discovered a magic cure. I understand why people would feel that way. But, what if I told you that none of those negative thoughts matters, that you can rewire your mind and beliefs to achieve what we have? As long as you have the slightest desire for the two of you to stay married, you can attain that goal. Imagine this scenario: a few years from now, you look back and can't remember why you wanted to leave your marriage in the first place?

Why do I believe in healed marriages? I was there, where you are right now, at the bottom of that valley. I found a way to change course and climb the mountain. I believe because our marriage was healed!

Let's be clear. Your journey will not be easy and sometimes, life will not yield to your expectation. I learned a hard lesson in Brazilian Ju-Jitsu; when it seems like you have an advantage, you can still lose the fight. In competition, even after mounting your opponent, you can make a minute mistake that will trip you up and force you into submission. I discovered that I don't have to win every battle, nor make every decision perfectly, to make it up to the top.

Even with all my knowledge and experience, I am continually battling the thoughts that pop into my head every day. Not all of them will be detrimental to my marriage. But as explained before, the smallest mistakes can cause you to slip, fall, and become buried in a crevasse. You must get your thoughts in order to make a successful climb up the marriage mountain.

I have made it to the summit and I can tell you, it's a beautiful sight to see. I fought through the negativity and resistance and can now focus on love instead of problems. I began this journey as an inexperienced partner; I became a life coach and motivational speaker. This may not be your future, but somewhere down the road, you will cross paths with a couple who are struggling in their marriage. Once you have read this book and been educationally equipped to give advice, you can help them. What a wonderful feeling to share from your heart and bring two people back to a healthy marriage! Tia and I hope you share this book and encourage more couples to become part of the Mountaineer Marriage community.

For those who decide to travel up Marriage Mountain with us, I encourage you to write down your goals for your marriage. Before or after you say, "I do," create a plan for you and your partner so you can be intentional and enjoy a lifelong journey!

Conclusion

The Expedition
Don't focus solely on the mountain. Understand the journey and become familiar with the process.

Learn The Mountain
Just because "Marriage Mountain" looks exciting to climb, without proper education, you are endangered of creating bad habits. Educate yourself, have patience, and remember to be consistent.

Gearing Up
Make sure you have the proper tools and understanding that will set your marriage up for success!

Dynamic Partnership
The more reliable the connection between you and your spouse, the stronger the marriage will be. Remember, treat your marriage as if life depended on your ability to have a strong partnership.

The Climb
For a Mountaineer, endurance is everything. Prepare yourself mentally and physically, so you will have what it takes to be resilient!

Stay On Route
There is a right way, a hard way, and a wrong way. The proper path is laid out in front of you. Stay focus and constantly seek the will of God.

The Killer Crevasse
Rock bottom is a difficult place to be. Remember the four stages to prevent from making damaging mistakes.

The Fighting Purpose
The "purpose" is a crucial component in creating a fulfilling life. Seek God's will, and he will give your marriage a divine purpose.

Ice-SAR Rescue
If you understand the journey, you will have the knowledge needed to help another couple who is climbing up marriage mountain. Remember, your challenges will become your testimonies.

The Summit
Enjoy the view, but know that you can't stay on top of the summit for long. We must continuously keep moving so we can grow. But always have gratitude toward your accomplishments!

Mountaineer Marriage LLC

MOUNTAINEER MARRIAGE

Contact us at
www.mountaineermarriage.com
if you are in need of
marriage coaching

ABOUT THE AUTHOR

D. Deshazer

DeShazer is a family man first, with a wife and two beautiful daughters. As a film producer, musician, and author, his passion for influencing the world has put him in the position to become somewhat of an educator. Through life's experiences and a willingness to positively impact others' lives, DeShazer was blessed to be given a platform to become a public figure. As a content creator, DeShazer is able to reach out to a wide range of demographics and personalities and is proving to become an inspiration that will never be forgotten.

Made in the USA
Columbia, SC
31 July 2020